Gospel Fun Ac

Quick-and-Easy Family Home
and Sharing Time Presentations

- Scripture Lessons
- Bite-size Memorize Scriptures
- Learning Games and Activities
- Thought Treats

A-Z Gospel Subjects

Accountability Choose the Right Commandments

Faith Follow Jesus Holy Ghost

Missionary Talents Missionary Work Repentance

Second Coming Service Testimony

Introducing the Author and Illustrator, Creators of the

Primary Partners series, *Young Women Fun-tastic!* series, *Gospel Fun Activities, Super Singing Activities, File Folder Family Home Evenings*, and *Home-spun Fun Family Home Evenings* series, found in books and CD-ROMs

MARY H. ROSS, Author

Mary Ross is an energetic mother, and has been a Primary teacher and Achievement Days leader. She loves to help children and young women have a good time while they learn. She has studied acting, modeling, and voice. Her varied interests include writing, creating activities and children's parties, and cooking. Mary and her husband, Paul, live with their daughter, Jennifer, in Sandy, Utah.

JENNETTE GUYMON-KING, Illustrator

Jennette Guymon-King has studied graphic arts and illustration at Utah Valley State College and the University of Utah. She served a mission to Japan. Jennette enjoys sports, reading, cooking, art, gardening, and freelance illustrating. Jennette and her husband, Clayton, live in Riverton, Utah. They are the proud parents of their daughter Kayla Mae, and sons Levi and Carson.

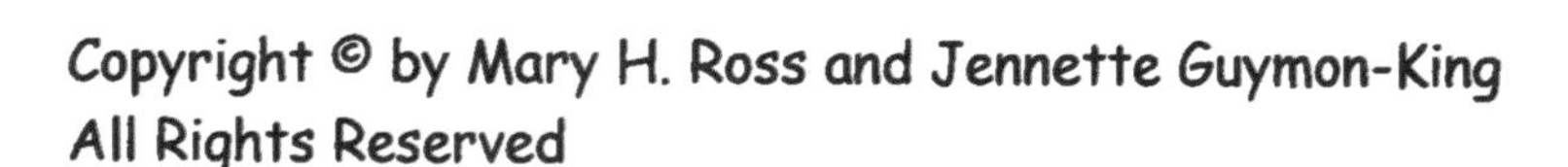

Covenant Communications, Inc.
American Fork, Utah

Printed in China
First Printing: October 2002

Gospel Fun Activities: Quick-and-Easy Family Home Evenings
ISBN: 1-59156-054-3

ACKNOWLEDGMENTS: Thanks to Inspire Graphics (www.inspiregraphics.com)for the use of Lettering Delights computer fonts.

INTRODUCTION

Gospel Fun Activities

Quick-and-Easy
Family Home Evenings and Sharing Time Presentations

In minutes you can teach a child basic principles of the gospel from the games and activities in this book. As a picture is worth 1,000 words, we have created the visuals that will help you teach the gospel with very little effort. These teaching tools are easy to present on a poster, board, or on the wall. Children enjoy creating and presenting the activities, so put them in charge whenever you can.

These *Gospel Fun Activities* are ideal for family home evening and Primary sharing time. Parents can use the activities and thought treats to simplify family home evening lessons and make learning fun. Primary leaders and teachers can use the ideas to create sharing time presentations and add to lessons.

The visuals are ready-to-use to post and present, helping you teach important Gospel subjects: Accountability, Choose the Right, Commandments, Faith, Follow Jesus, The Holy Ghost, Missionary Talents, Missionary Work, Repentance, Second Coming, Service, and Testimony.

HERE'S HOW TO USE THIS BOOK:

1. Prepare the Quick-and-Easy Visuals:
Simply tear out the already colored images from the perforated pages, cut out the visuals, and use.
If you want to prepare the visuals for durability to be used again and again, prepare according to the instructions on the last page of this Introduction.

2. *Assign Family Home Evening Responsibilities:*

Your family will hop on over to a fun family evening as you use this frog family chart to assign responsibilities.

TO MAKE:

1. Mount the family home evening chart on a poster paper (unless you are planning to decoupage images onto wood).
2. Cut out the images.
3. Write the name of a family member on each frog, writing the father's name on the large frog and the mother's name of the frog with the ribbon.
4. Laminate chart and frogs for durability.
5. Attach frogs onto lily pads with sticky-back velcro or tape.

To Display: Post on a refrigerator by adding sticky-back magnets to the back, or post on a bulletin board using tacks or T-pins.

TO USE:

At the end of family home evening, make your assignments for the next week by moving the frogs to the responsibility on the chart, e.g., lesson or activity, scripture, music.

3. *Motivate Scripture Memorization:*

Use the scripture Bite-size Memorize posters and cards (shown right) to help children memorize important scriptures.

4. *Prepare Treats:*

Purchase ingredients to make *Thought Treats* before family home evening (may not be appropriate for sharing time).

5. *Present the Gospel Fun Activity:*

Use the visuals to teach using the lesson plan and ideas given at the beginning of each activity.

TO PRINT IMAGES:

All images can be printed in color or black and white, using the *Gospel Fun Activities* CD-ROM (shown right). See the back cover of this book.

To Prepare the Visuals to Be Used Again and Again:

The purpose of this book is to provide you with easy-to-use visuals. With the following tools and methods, you can produce visuals that can be used again and again. For durability, these visuals should be mounted on a heavier backing and then laminated. You will find that mounting the visuals on cardstock or poster paper increases the durability, and keeps the visuals rigid for easier posting on the board, walls, or poster for display purposes.
TOOLS: *You'll Need:* Artist's spray adhesive (best and quickest), glue, or rubber cement, cardstock or poster paper, scissors.

TO MOUNT VISUALS ON CARDSTOCK OR POSTER PAPER:

1. *Mounting Two-Part Visuals:* Tape them together on the back before mounting.
2. *Mounting Visuals:* Before cutting out the visual, spray the entire back of the visual using the artist's spray adhesive (best results), or evenly spread the glue or rubber cement over the entire visual and stick visual to your choice of rigid backing (cardstock or poster paper). Glues will require drying time before laminating or cutting out, but spray adhesive is ready immediately. Once the visual is stuck to the backing, you are now ready for cutting or laminating.
3. *Laminating Your Visuals:* Laminating increases the durability of your visuals and allows you to use the visuals over and over without tearing.
4. *Laminate Posters:* Consider laminating several large posters front and back to create a smooth surface. Then when you post the visuals, the tape won't tear or mar the poster paper.
5. *Laminating with a Machine:* Laminating done with a machine is the most durable, but it is not necessary. Clear Contact paper also creates a laminate surface. If you are machine laminating your visuals, cut them out first and then laminate. Once the visuals are laminated, cut the laminate 1/8th of an inch or more from the edge of the visual to keep the edges from separating from the lamination.
6. *Laminating with Clear Contact Paper:* If you are laminating your visuals using clear Contact paper, glue them to the backing first and then laminate. Cut the Contact paper the size needed to cover the visual. Separate the backing on one end of the Contact paper only a few inches. Position the Contact paper over the visual and as you slowly remove the backing, press the Contact paper on the visual to avoid any bubbles or creases. Repeat on the back of the visual and then cut out.

STORING YOUR VISUALS:

1. *Manila Folders:* Store visuals in a manila folder so that they will remain flat and away from the sun to prevent bending and the colors from fading.
2. *Larger Folders:* If you have larger visuals that will bend if placed in a manila folder, make a large folder using poster paper. Fold the poster in half and tape the left and right sides, leaving the top open.

Table of Contents

Introduction
"Hop on Over to Family Home Evening" Chart

Gospel Fun Activities Themes #1-12

#1 Accountability: I Am Responsible for My Choices (Annabell's Accountable Cow Farm) 1-18

#2 Choose the Right: I Will Let Heavenly Father Help Me Choose the Right (CTR Tools Choose the Right Match Game) 19-34

#3 Commandments: I Can Return to My Heavenly Father (Commandment Maze) 35-50

#4 Faith: My Faith Can Grow (Choices: Strong and Wilting Plant Match Game) 51-70

#5 Follow Jesus: I Will Always Remember Jesus (Find the Light: Situation Spotlight) 71-82

#6 Holy Ghost: The Holy Ghost Will Help Me Choose the Right (Trail to Holy Ghost Town Game) 83-104

#7 Missionary Talents: I Will Share the Gospel (Missionary Mystery Kite Maze) 105-122

#8 Missionary Work: I Can Be a Fisher of Men, Like Jesus (Missionary "Fish"-ionary Fish Find) 123-140

#9 Repentance: Repentance Can Make Us Happy (Happy Henry and Miserable Mac Body Building Puzzles) 141-158

#10 Second Coming: I Will Be Ready to Meet Jesus When He Comes Again (Second Coming Suitcase) 159-172

#11 Service: I Will Love and Serve Others (My Service Garden Game to Plan Acts of Service) . . . 173-192

#12 Testimony: I Will Build My House upon the Rock of Jesus Christ (Testimony Rocks to Build a Sure Foundation) 193-210

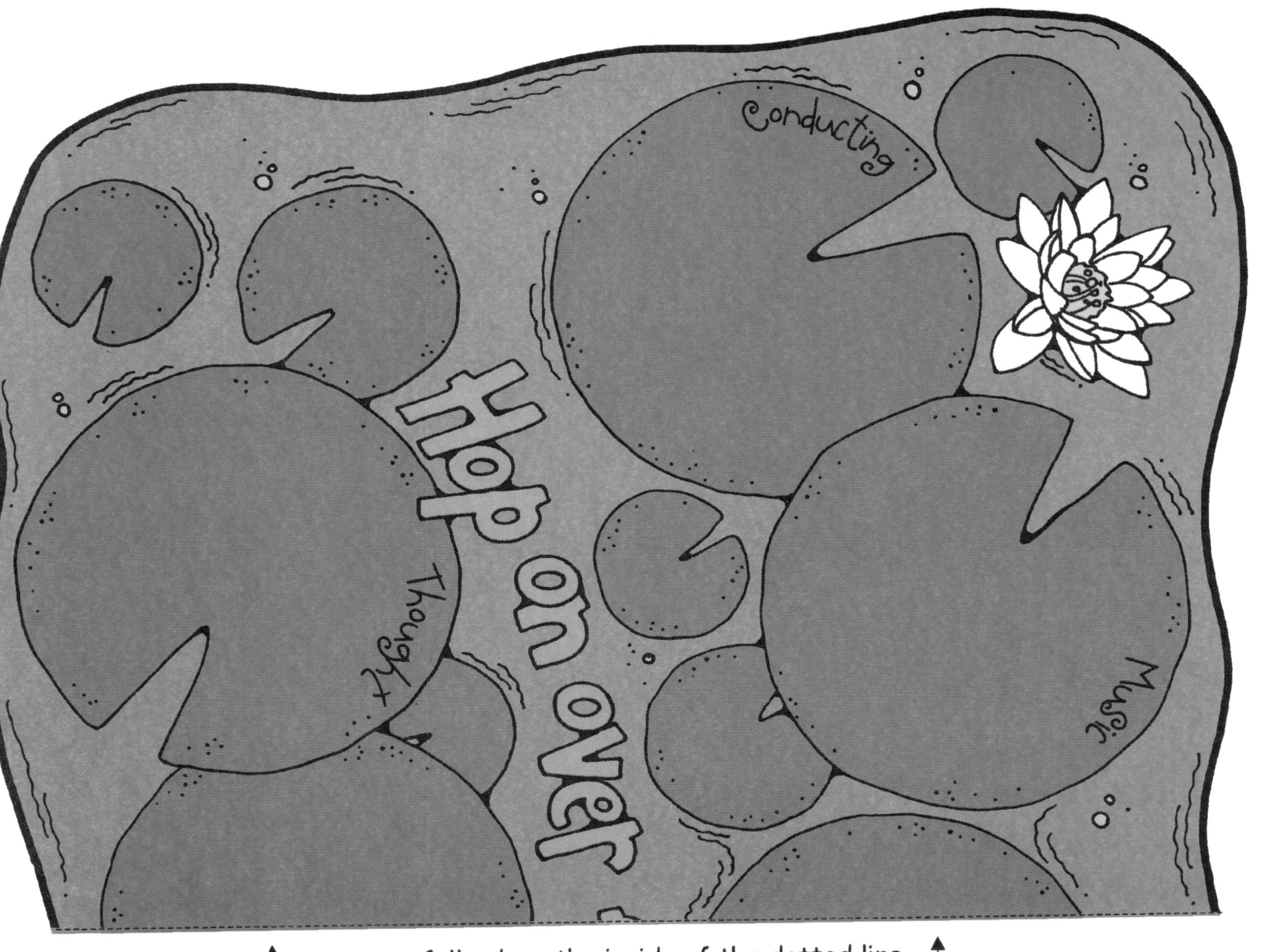

↑ Cut carefully along the inside of the dotted line. ↑

Do not cut on the dotted line. Use this margin to mount the other side.

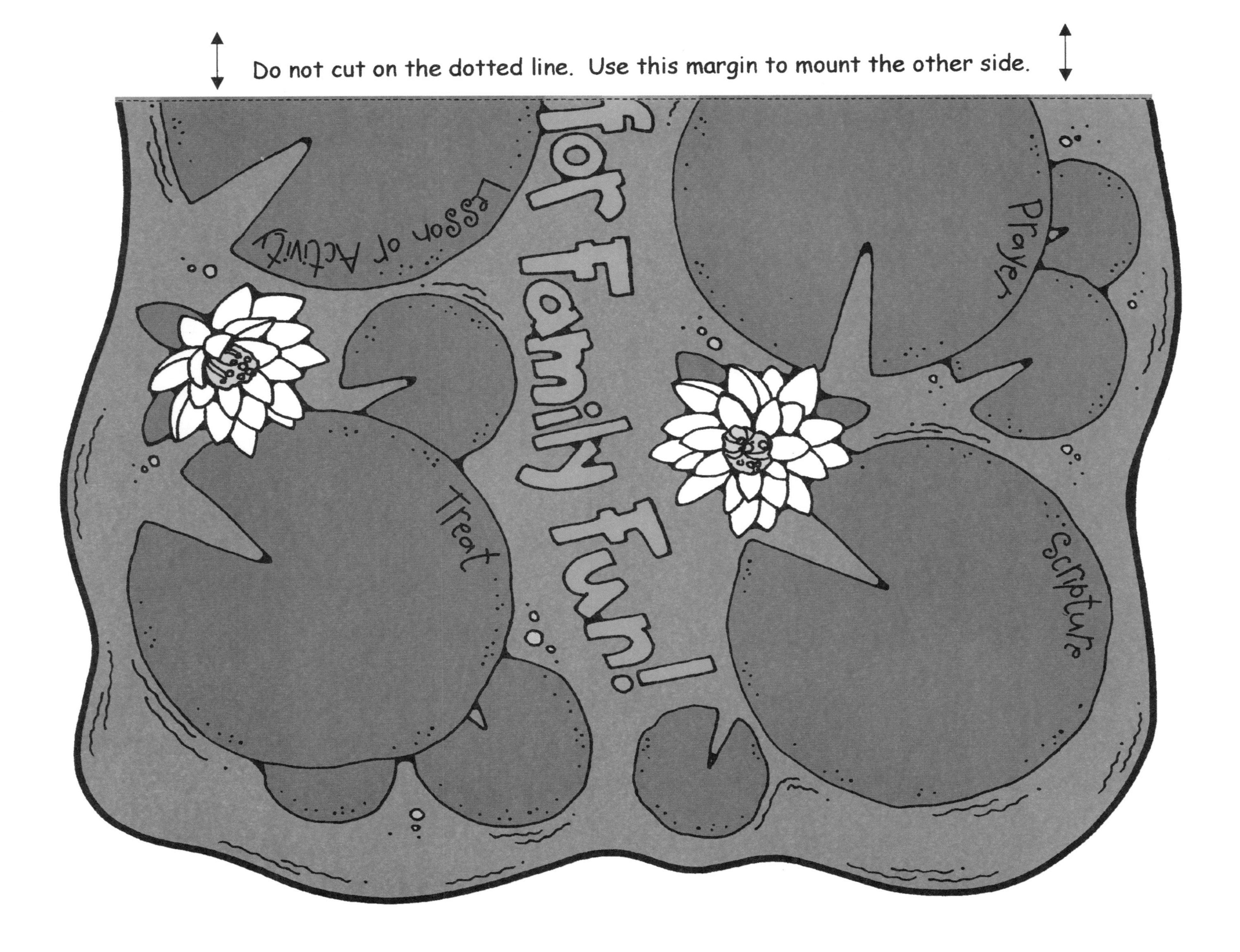

#1 – Accountability: I Am Responsible for My Choices

Scripture to Memorize: Memorize the D&C 68:27 scripture (shown right) on page 3.

Lesson Ideas:

PICTURE: Obtain picture of a child being baptized.
QUESTION: Ask "Why Is it Important for Me to Be Baptized When I Am Eight Years Old?" and answer the question using the scriptures and Primary lessons to teach.

#1: The Lord has set the age of eight years as the time when we begin to be accountable and can be baptized (Doctrine and Covenants 20:71; 29:47; *Primary 3—CTR B*, lesson 27).

#2: Being accountable means that we can tell the difference between right and wrong. We are responsible for our choices and actions (Moroni 8:8-10; *Primary 4—Book of Mormon*, lesson 24).

#3: When we are accountable, we repent and correct our wrong choices (Alma 36:5-24; *Primary 1—Nursery/Sunbeam*, lesson 29, *Primary 3—CTR B*, lesson 10).

ACTIVITY: I am Responsible for My Choices

(Annabell's Accountable Cow Farm)

OBJECTIVE: Help children learn the difference between right and wrong and learn to be responsible for their choices. We can be like the accountable cow who is "udder"ly responsible and "udder"ly prepared to be baptized. Talk about the different pastures the cows could go in. Inside the Peaceful Pasture the cow can find safety, food, and comfort. Inside the Dry Desert, the cow would find neither safety, food nor comfort. We want to be part of Heavenly Father's kingdom where we will find peace and happiness. As we choose the right, we can find our Peaceful Pasture.

TO MAKE:

1. Mount the barn top and bottom as follows on cardstock paper, laminate, and cut out.
2. Tape the top half of the barn on the board or a large poster, e.g., a green poster with the barn to the far left so that the green pasture is only on the right. Tape the bottom half of the barn on the board or poster to create a pocket leaving the top open to enclose cows.
3. Mount the cows and fence as follows on cardstock paper, laminate and cut out.
4. Place Peaceful Pasture fence on the right (symbolizing Choose the Right) and Dry Desert fence on the left.
5. Place all cows in the barn pocket to draw from.

INTRODUCE GAME: Tell children that we were sent to earth to learn to be responsible (to make right choices). By the time we are eight years old we are accountable, or responsible for our choices. We can be baptized at eight and be forgiven of our sins. At this time we receive the gift of the Holy Ghost to guide us in choosing the right. We can be more responsible now that we have the Holy Ghost to guide us. If we make mistakes after baptism, we need to repent and change wrong choices to right choices. Let's learn what it means to be accountable by placing the accountable cows in Annabell's Accountable Cow Farm. We can learn to be responsible for our decisions and place the cow that made the right decisions in Peaceful Pasture, and the cows that made the wrong decisions in the Dry Desert. If the cow repents and changes his actions from wrong to right, he can move into the Peaceful Pasture.

TO PLAY:

1. Divide children into two teams.
2. Teams take turns pulling a cow out of the barn, reading the words on the cow.
3. If the cow made a responsible decision by choosing the right, place the cow in the Peaceful Pasture and collect 2 points. If the cow did not choose the right, place him in the Dry Desert without collecting a point.
4. New players can either take a new cow out of the barn and take a chance on pulling out a cow that did not choose the right. Or, they can choose a cow out of the Dry Dessert and tell how the cow can repent and make a responsible decision (choosing the right). They can then place the repentant cow in the Peaceful Pasture and collect 2 points.
5. The team with the most points wins after all the cows are out of the barn and the Dry Desert.

THOUGHT TREAT (when appropriate): Serve cow treats (ice cream, yogurt). Say that cows are very special animals and give so much to us in providing milk, cheese, butter, and meat. They are responsible for helping us in this way. We too can be responsible to serve others and make right choices.

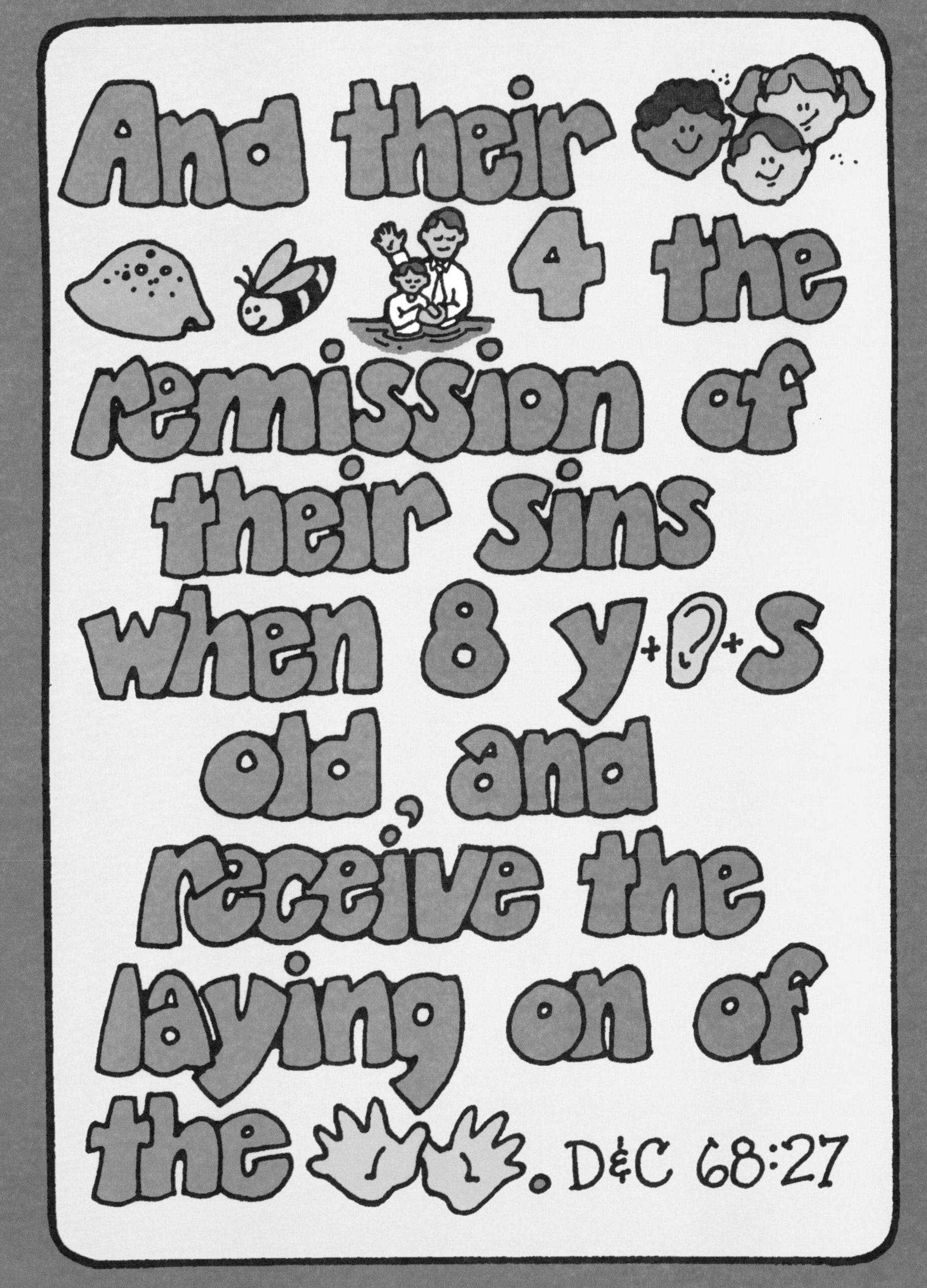
BITE SIZE MEMORIZE
And their
4 the
remission of
their sins
when 8 y s
old, and
receive the
laying on of
the
D&C 68:27

↑ Cut carefully along the inside of the dotted line. ↑

↑ Cut carefully along the inside of the dotted line. ↑

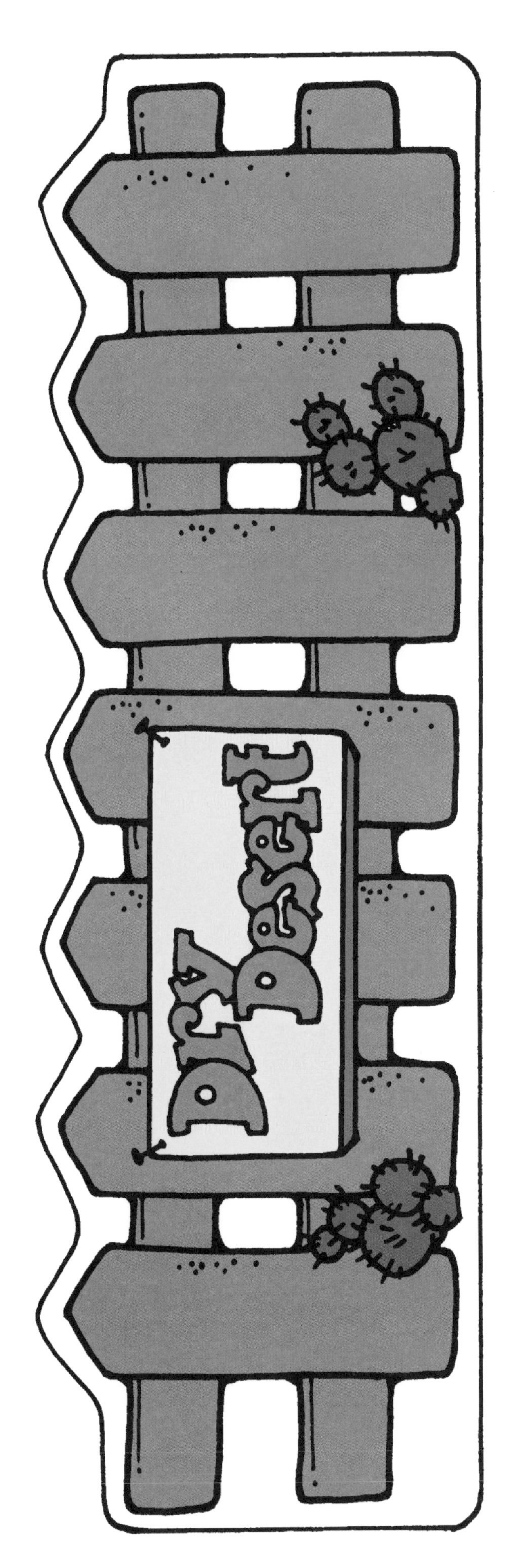
Dry Desert

Peaceful Pasture

My friend wanted me to watch a movie I didn't feel good about, so I said "no."
Someone asked me to swear. I told him I didn't care to swear.
At night I get real tired and think I don't have time to pray, but I pray anyway.
My friends said that a girl was weird. I said, "I like her."
My parents don't like to listen to Conference, but I turn on the TV and listen anyway.
My parents don't have to ask me if I cleaned my room. I try to always keep it clean.
My mother doesn't need to remind me to practice my music.
Dad asked me to return something to a neighbor. I forgot, but then I returned it.

I told my brother "I'm sorry" when I hurt his feelings.
I go to Church on Sunday so I can choose the right on Monday.
I was eating my favorite treat when a friend came up. I decided to share.
I listened to and read to an elderly person who was lonely.
I try to be a missionary by being a friend.
I said something mean to a friend.
I took something that did not belong to me.
A friend asked me about church and I didn't invite him to come with me.

I told Mother I would be home at 5:00 and I was 5 minutes early.
I was tempted to spend my tithing but didn't.
The family didn't have scripture study so I read on my own.
My friend asked me to play on Sunday but I took her to Primary instead.
I liked my friend's ring, but I didn't take it.
It was time for the sacrament so I thought about Jesus.
My friend was talking to me in Primary and I chose to be reverent.
I started thinking about my birthday party at church, but I decided to listen to my teacher.

I thought about my vacation during the sacrament.
I was unkind to my younger brother.
Dad asked me to rake the leaves and I went to play instead.
I could see my neighbor needed help shoveling his walk and I didn't help.
I learned about someone in need and I didn't pray for them.
My friends asked me to play a joke on the teacher, so I helped.
I broke a neighbor's window while hitting the baseball. Then I ran away.
The store man gave me too much change and I kept the money.

#2 – Choose the Right:

I Will Let Heavenly Father Help Me Choose the Right

Scripture to Memorize: Memorize the Psalm 119:105 scripture (shown right) on page 21.

Lesson Ideas:

QUESTION: Ask "*What other special helps has Heavenly Father given us to help us keep our baptismal covenant?*" and answer the question using the scriptures, Primary lessons to teach.

#1: Our parents, teachers, and leaders help us (1 Nephi 3:7; Mosiah 4:14-15; Doctrine and Covenants 68:25-28; *Primary 1,* lesson 43; *Primary 3,* lessons 8, 28; *Primary 4,* lessons 27, 29).

#2: The scriptures help us (Matthew 4:4; 2 Timothy 3:16; 1 Nephi 19:23; 2 Nephi 4:15-16; Doctrine and Covenants 84:57; *Primary 1,* lesson 41; *Primary 4,* lesson 23; *Primary 6,* lesson 37).

#3: Prayer and fasting help us (2 Nephi 32:9; Doctrine and Covenants 10:5; 19:38; 88:119; *Primary 1,* lesson 4, *Primary 6,* lessons 38, 42 *Primary 7, lesson 11).*

ACTIVITY: I Will Use Special Helps Heavenly Father Has Given Me to Choose the Right

(Ctr Tool Choose-and-match)

OBJECTIVE: Help children recognize tools or special helps that Heavenly Father has given them to keep their baptismal covenants and to keep the commandments.

TO MAKE:

1. Mount CTR Tools box (pages 23, 25) on cardstock paper, laminate and cut out. Cut a slit on the dashed lines.

2. Tape tool box on the board or mount to poster, taping or gluing the sides only, leaving the slit pocket open.
4. Mount tools (pages 27-32) on cardstock paper, laminate and cut out. Place tools in the pocket of the tool box.
5. Cut up wordstrips (page 33) and place in a container.

ACTIVITY:
1. Tell children that Heavenly Father has given us special helps or tools to help us choose the right and keep our baptismal covenant, e.g., PARENTS, TEACHERS, LEADERS, SCRIPTURES, PRAYER, and FASTING. Show tools in the CTR Tools box.
2. Have children come up one at a time and draw a problem wordstrip and read it.

3. Have children decide which tools they would use to help them keep their baptismal covenant and keep the commandments.
4. Ask children to tell why they chose the tool or tools and how they will help fix the problem.
5. Have each child place the wordstrip in a separate container and place tools back into the CTR Tools box.

THOUGHT TREAT (when appropriate): CTR Wafer Cookies. Write the letters CTR on a wafer cookie using a tube of frosting for each child. Tell children that CTR tools will help us keep our baptismal covenants. There is a gate that leads to the strait and narrow path that leads to heaven. Baptism is the gate. After baptism we are on the strait and narrow path. If we continue using the CTR tools, e.g., reading the scriptures, listening to parents and teachers, and fasting and praying we can stay on the path and find happiness in our journey.

BITE SIZE MEMORIZE

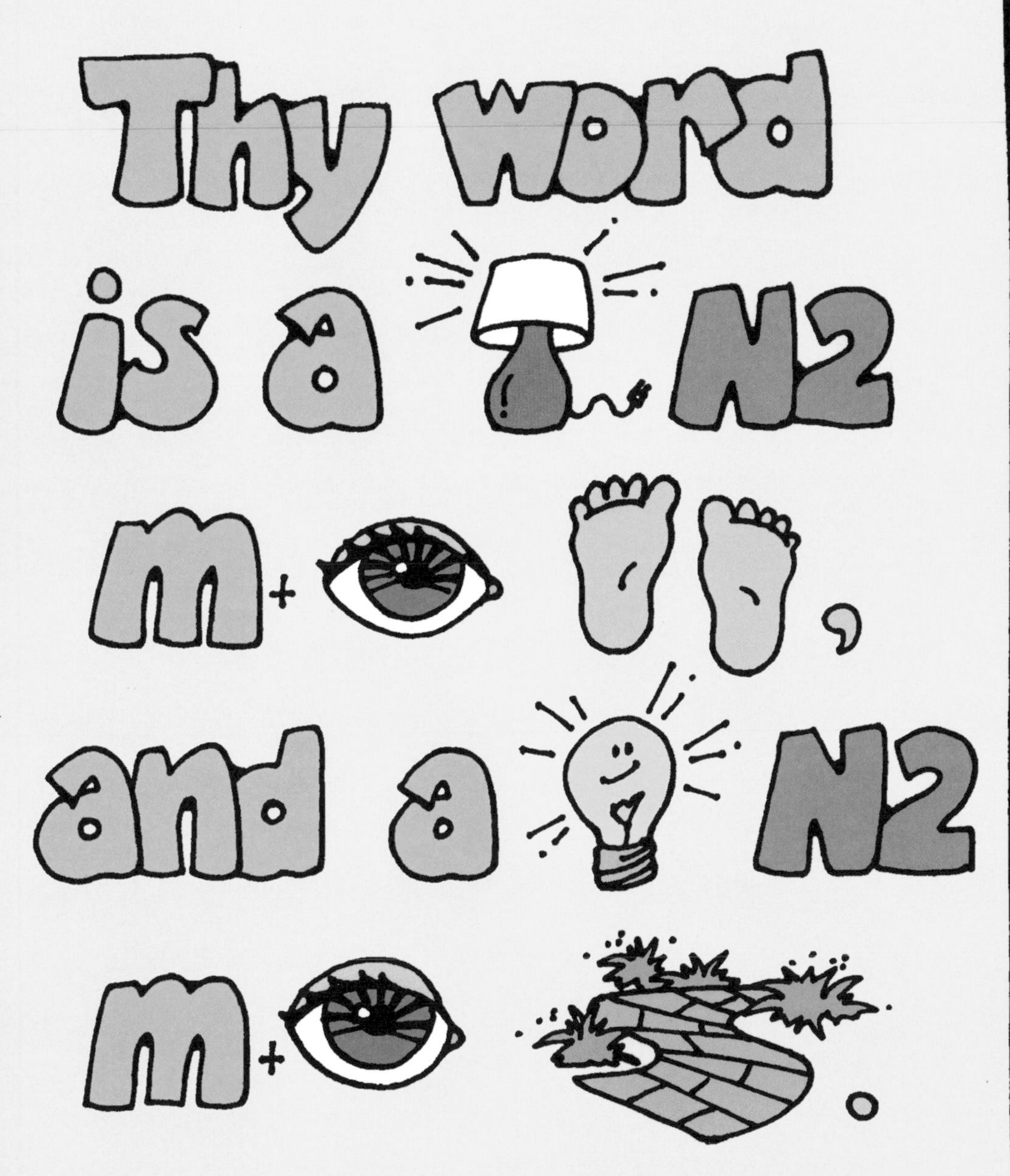

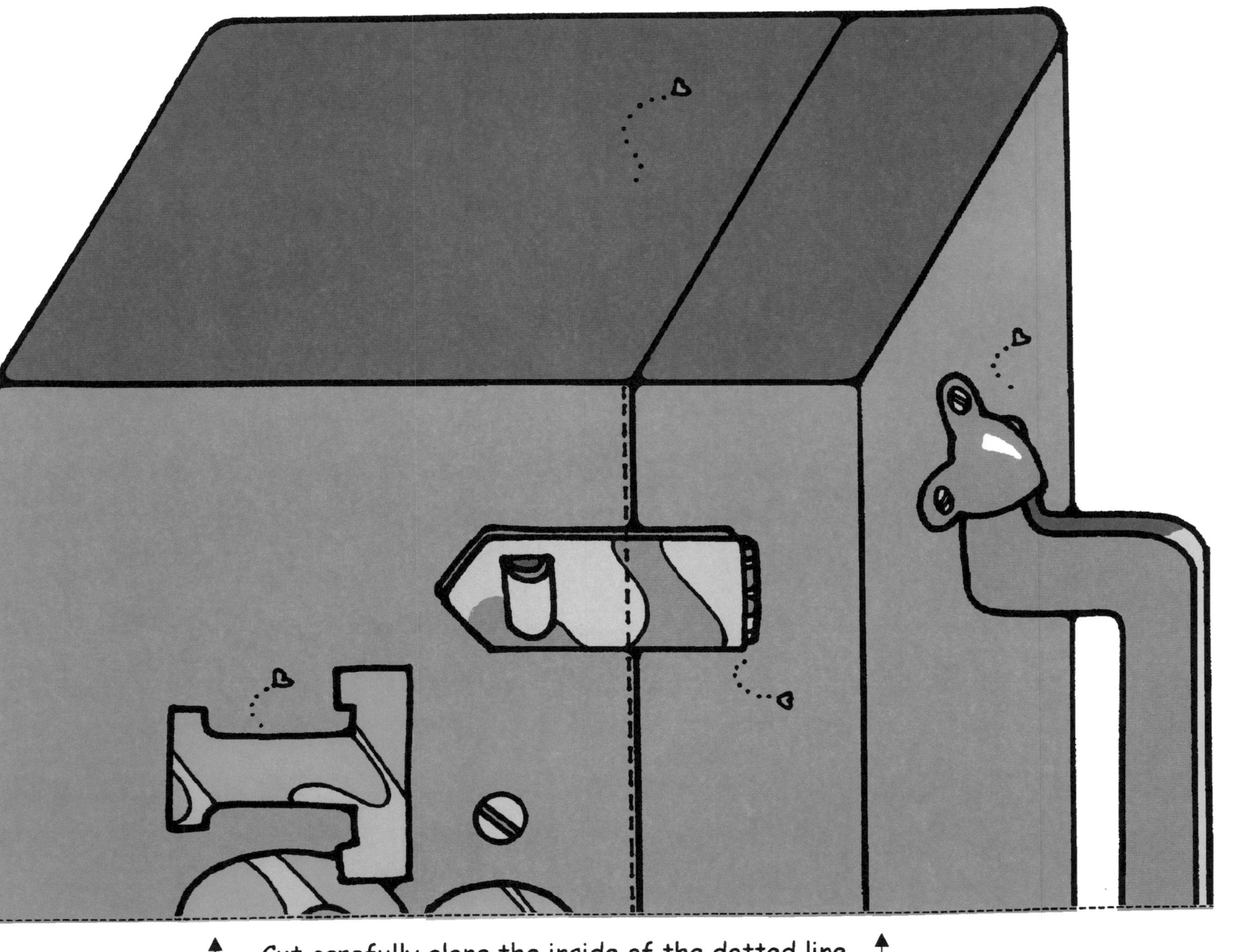

↑ Cut carefully along the inside of the dotted line. ↑

Do not cut on the dotted line. Use this margin to mount the other side.

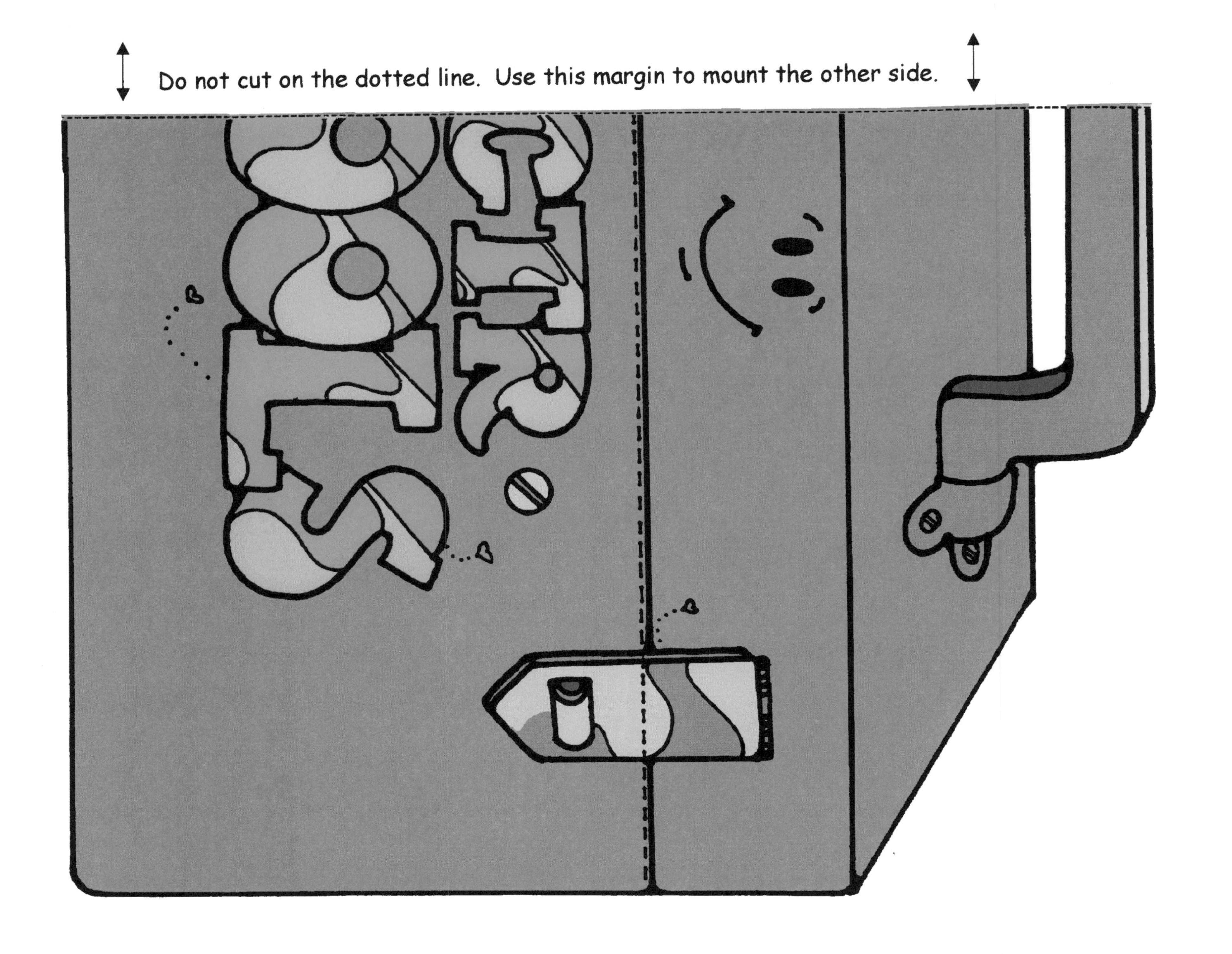

Leaders

1 2 3 4 5 6
Leaders

Parents
Fasting

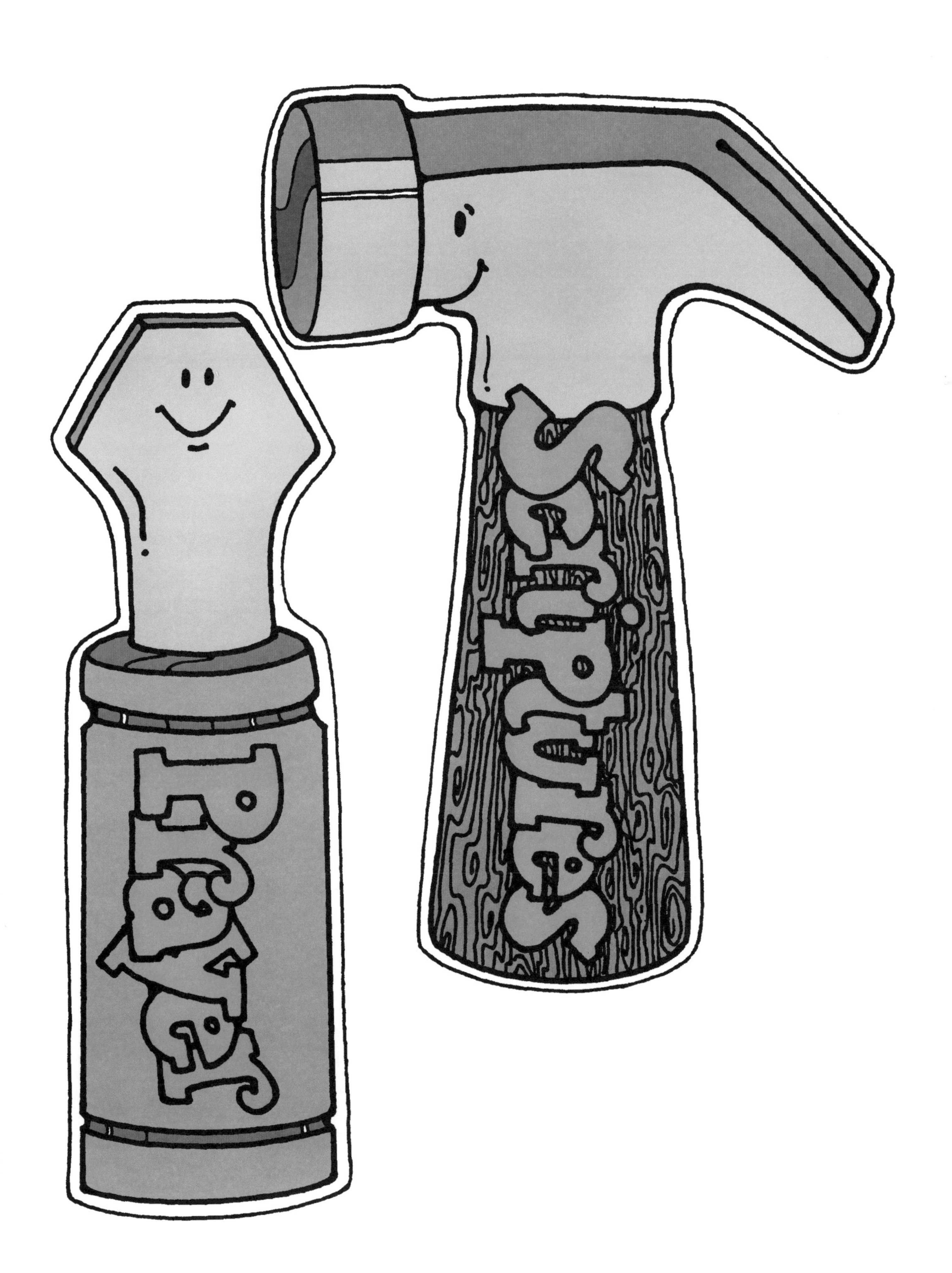
Prayer
Scriptures

Kim rode her friend's new bike without asking and she ran into a fence and bent the front wheel. Which tool?

Chaz was afraid to go to school where two boys were unkind to him. Which tool?

Liz wanted to sing in the Primary choir but she didn't think she could sing very well or learn the words. Which tool?

Lisa wanted learn about babysitting so that she could be a good babysitter when she is asked to babysit. Which tool?

Chip wanted to to to church on Sunday but his parents didn't go. Which tool?
Caroline wanted to be baptized but her parents didn't want her to be baptized. Which tool?

Alexa wanted to learn how to play the piano so she could someday play at church. Which tool?

Nathan went out into the forest and didn't know which way to go to get back to camp. Which tool?

Malorie wanted to invite a friend to come to church but she was afraid to ask. Which tool?

Maddy wanted her parents to be married in the temple so she could be sealed to them for eternity. Which tool?

Erick's grandpa was very sick and Stan was very worried that he might die. Which tool?

Nick had a spelling bee and he forgot to study the words. Which tool?

Kristen wanted to play with a friend after school that she didn't think her mother would like. Which tool?

Jessie wanted a necklace at the store and she didn't have enough money to pay for it. Which tool?

Jeff always came straight home from school, but Travis asked him to go to the store to buy candy. Which tool?

Kara's friend liked to drink beer when she was at her house. She asked Kara if she wanted some. Which tool?

Jenny wanted to know if the Book of Mormon was true. Which tool?

Camille liked this girl at school, but her friends kept saying what they didn't like about her. Which tool?

Levi liked to ride horses and his friend asked him if he wanted to ride his horses on Sunday. Which tool?

Branden liked to play video games. Many times his mother asked him to do something and he pretended he didn't hear. Which tool?

Brady threw a frisbee in the house and broke his mother's new lamp. Which tool?

Bret couldn't see the writing on the blackboard but he didn't like to wear his new glasses. Which tool?

Marcus wanted to be a missionary to his next door neighbor but he didn't know how. Which tool?

Danny liked to think about heroes but he didn't know which hero he wanted to be like. Which tool?

Cindy noticed that the leaves were falling off the tree and she didn't know why. Which tool?

Mindy wanted to surprise her mother with breakfast in bed but didn't know how to fix breakfast. Which tool?

Justin wanted to gain a testimony. Which tool?

Mike wanted to learn about Nephi. Which tool?

Sue wanted to know why she should pay tithing. Which tool?

Tasha wanted to know what she should do when she saw someone in need. Which tool?

Megan had a problem she didn't know how to solve. Which tool?

Amberly wanted to live the "Gospel Standards" but didn't know what they were. Which tool?

Wendy wanted to know the Articles of Faith so she could tell her friend what we believe. Which tool?

Aubrey wanted to increase her faith. Which tool?

Camie couldn't sleep at night because she was worried about what she should do say if her friend asked her about the gospel. Which tool?

#3 – Commandments: I Can Return to My Heavenly Father

Scripture to Memorize: Memorize the John 14:15 scripture (shown right) on page 37.

Lesson Ideas:

QUESTIONS: Ask children the following questions using the scriptures and Primary lessons to teach. Tell children that Jesus Christ will help us to keep his commandments when we do these things.

#1: What are some of the commandments that we are asked to obey?

- Ten Commandments (Mosiah 12:32-37, D&C 42:18-28, Exodus 20:3-17),
- Love Others (D&C 59:5, Moses 6:33, D&C 42:29, D&C 4:2-4, Matthew 22:36-40, D&C 59:6),
- Laws of the Land (D&C 58:21, Alma 53:18-22),
- Fast (D&C 59:14, Moroni 6:5).

#2: When do we pray? (D&C 59:14, 1 Thessalonians 5:17-23, *Primary 1,* lesson 4, *Primary 2,* lesson 18, *Primary 3,* lesson 34, *Primary 5,* lesson 6, *Primary 4,* lesson 37)

#3: When do we study the scriptures? The scriptures testify of Jesus Christ (*Primary 1,* lesson 41, *Primary 5,* lesson 20, *Primary 6,* lesson 37, *Primary 7,* lesson 1, *Primary 4,* lesson 23, D&C 26:1, 2 Nephi 4:15, 3 Nephi 10:14, Matthew 22:29, Moses 1:39)

#4: What can we do to keep the Sabbath day holy? (Isaiah 56:1-8, D&C 68:29, *Primary 2,* lesson 37, *Primary 3,* lesson 40, *Primary 5,* lesson 41, *Primary 7,* lesson 14)

#5: Why do we pay tithing? (Proverbs 3:9, Mosiah 18:27-28, D&C 64:23; 85:3, Malachi 3:8-12, 3 Nephi 24:8-10)

#6: Why do we go to church and take the sacrament? (D&C 20:37; 75, Mosiah 18:6-10, D&C 19:23-24, Hebrews 9:28; 13:12, Mosiah 3:5-8, John 19:16-20, Mosiah 4:1-2, Alma 42:14-15, 2 Nephi 2:6-9, *Primary 3,* lesson 32 and 33, *Primary 1,* lesson 40, *Primary 4,* lesson 36)

ACTIVITY: I Can Return to My Heavenly Home

(Commandment Maze)

OBJECTIVE: Show children that as they obey the commandments they can find happiness and stay on the path that leads to life with Heavenly Father and Jesus Christ.

All images can be printed in color or black and white, using the *Gospel Fun Activities* CD-ROM.

TO MAKE:

1. Mount the START and FINISH signs (pages 39, 41), arrow, commandment signs, and number block (pages 43-50) on cardstock paper, laminate, and cut out.
2. Fold block and glue tabs inside.
3. Tape Jesus "FINISH" picture at the top of the board. Place commandment game pieces in any order below (between the FINISH and the START sign).

TO PLAY: Tell children, "We can return to our heavenly home to live with Heavenly Father and Jesus Christ if we obey the commandments. The commandments keep us on the path that leads to eternal life. If we get off the path, we need to repent and get back on the path. This way we will find peace and happiness."

1. Divide children into two teams, giving each team an arrow marker (team #1 or team #2), placing markers at the START position.
2. Teams take turns rolling block (die) to determine the number of moves on the path. The die could also read "roll again" or "lose a turn" to determine moves.

3. Throw the die to determine who moves first (the highest number starts first).
4. First team to play rolls the die and moves along the path the number of spaces rolled.
5. The child reads an action on commandment he or she lands on. The child then decides if the action is obeying the commandment or disobeying.
6. If they land on an obedient action, they can continue to move toward the finish line to win. If they land on a disobedient action, they must move their arrow back toward the start line—where they will begin their next turn. Once they land on an obedient action, they can turn their arrow around so they can move toward the finish line on their next turn. If they keep traveling in the wrong direction and go all the way to START, they can turn their arrow around and begin again.

Option for Older Children: Before playing, read Mosiah 4:6 and point to the Jesus FINISH sign and explain, "Because of Jesus and his atonement, we can gain exaltation by keeping his commandments. If we have faith in him, we can become like Jesus and FINISH our work here on this earth."

THOUGHT TREAT (when appropriate): Command "Mints". Give children/family some butter mints and tell them that Heavenly Father "mint" for us to live the commandments. This is why we were sent to earth, to prove that we can live Heavenly Father's laws and return to him. Name a commandment you want to keep for every mint you eat.

 All images can be printed in color or black and white, using the *Gospel Fun Activities* CD-ROM.

BITE SIZE MEMORIZE

John 14:15

ROLL AGAIN
1
2
3
4
LOSE A TURN

Was not kind to my brother.
Felt good enough to go to Primary, but didn't go.
Didn't help my grandmother when she asked me to.

START

FINISH

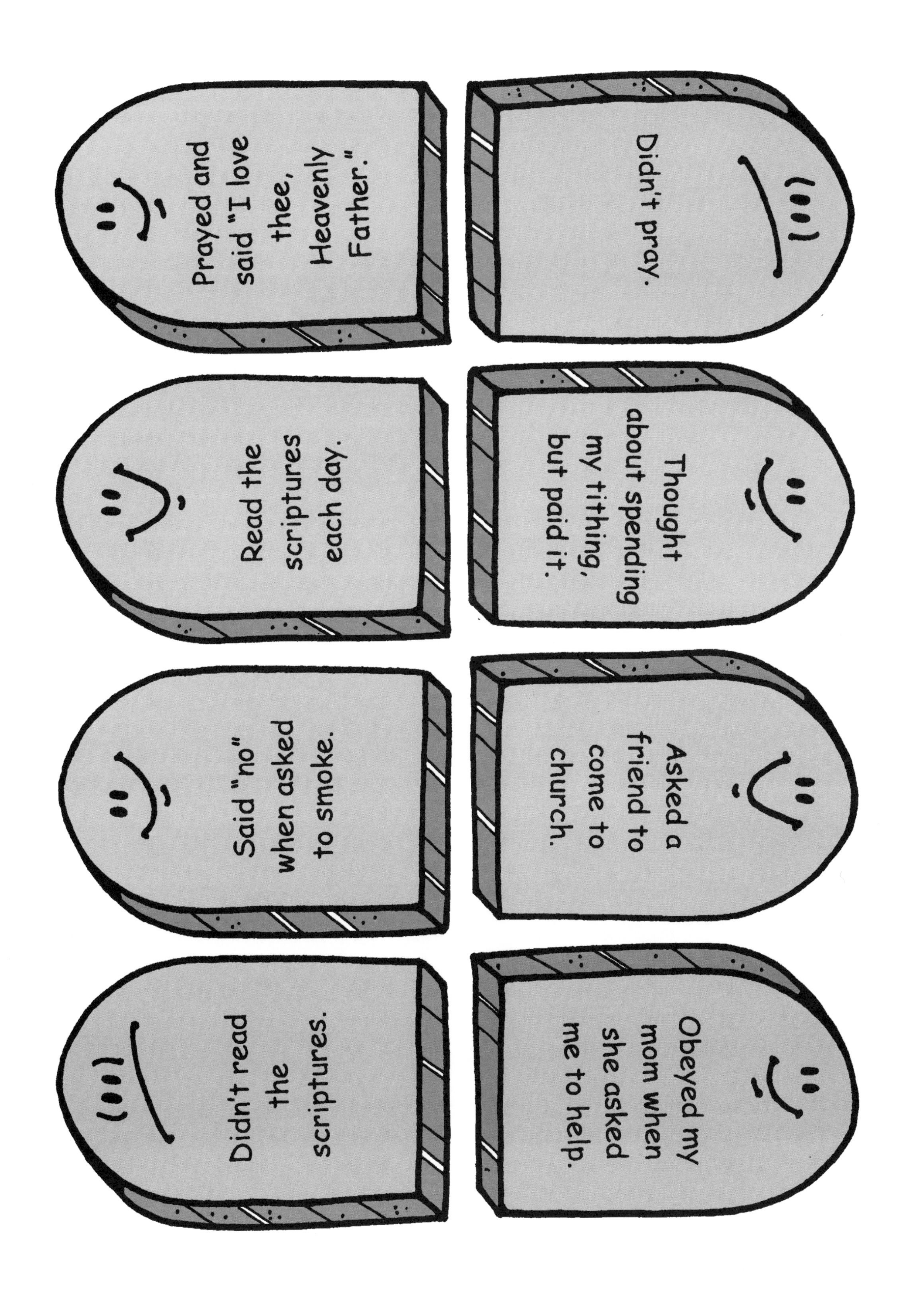
Prayed and said "I love thee, Heavenly Father."
Read the scriptures each day.
Said "no" when asked to smoke.
Didn't read the scriptures.
Didn't pray.
Thought about spending my tithing, but paid it.
Asked a friend to come to church.
Obeyed my mom when she asked me to help.

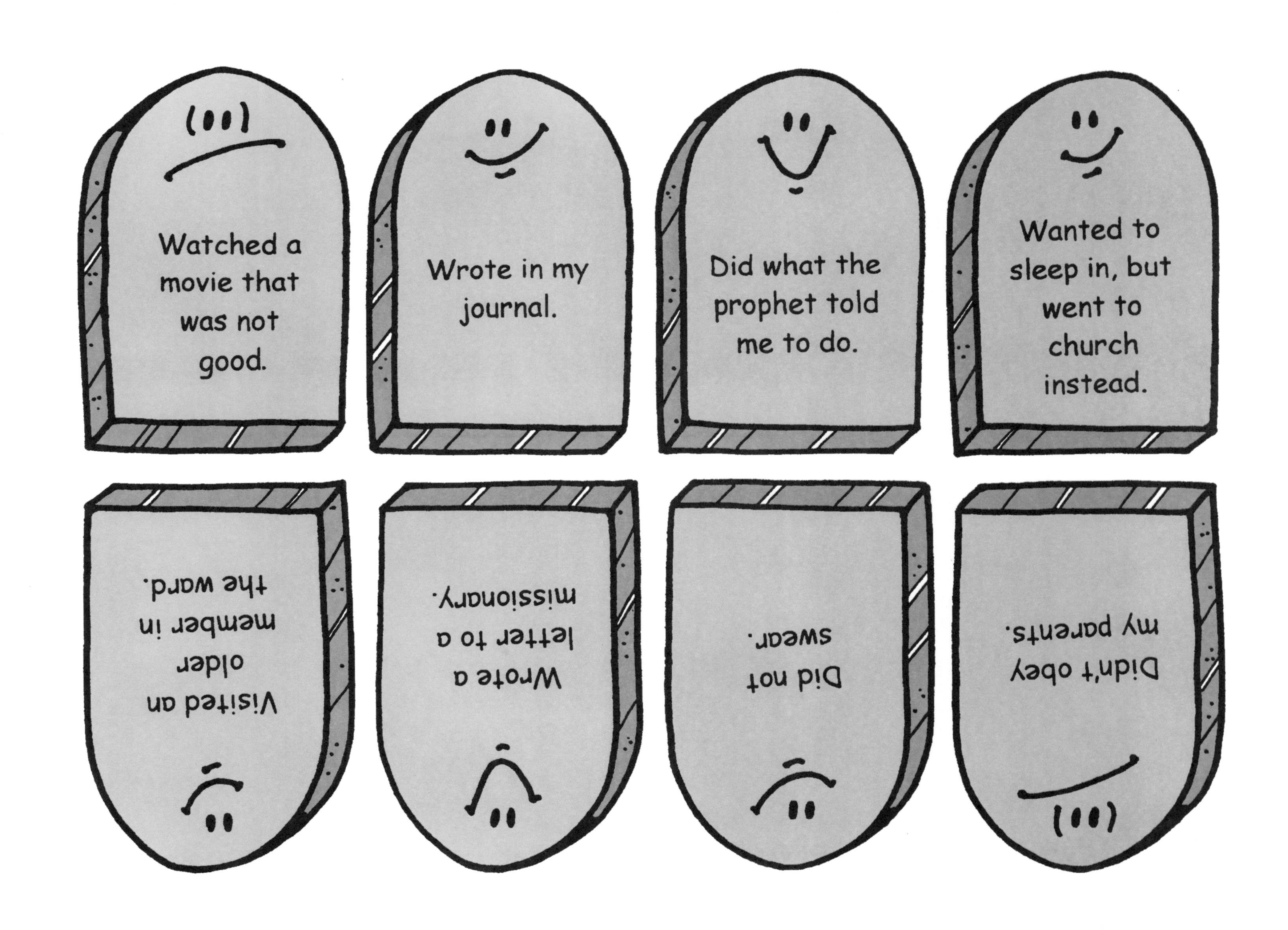
Watched a movie that was not good.
Wrote in my journal.
Did what the prophet told me to do.
Wanted to sleep in, but went to church instead.
Visited an older member in the ward.
Wrote a letter to a missionary.
Did not swear.
Didn't obey my parents.

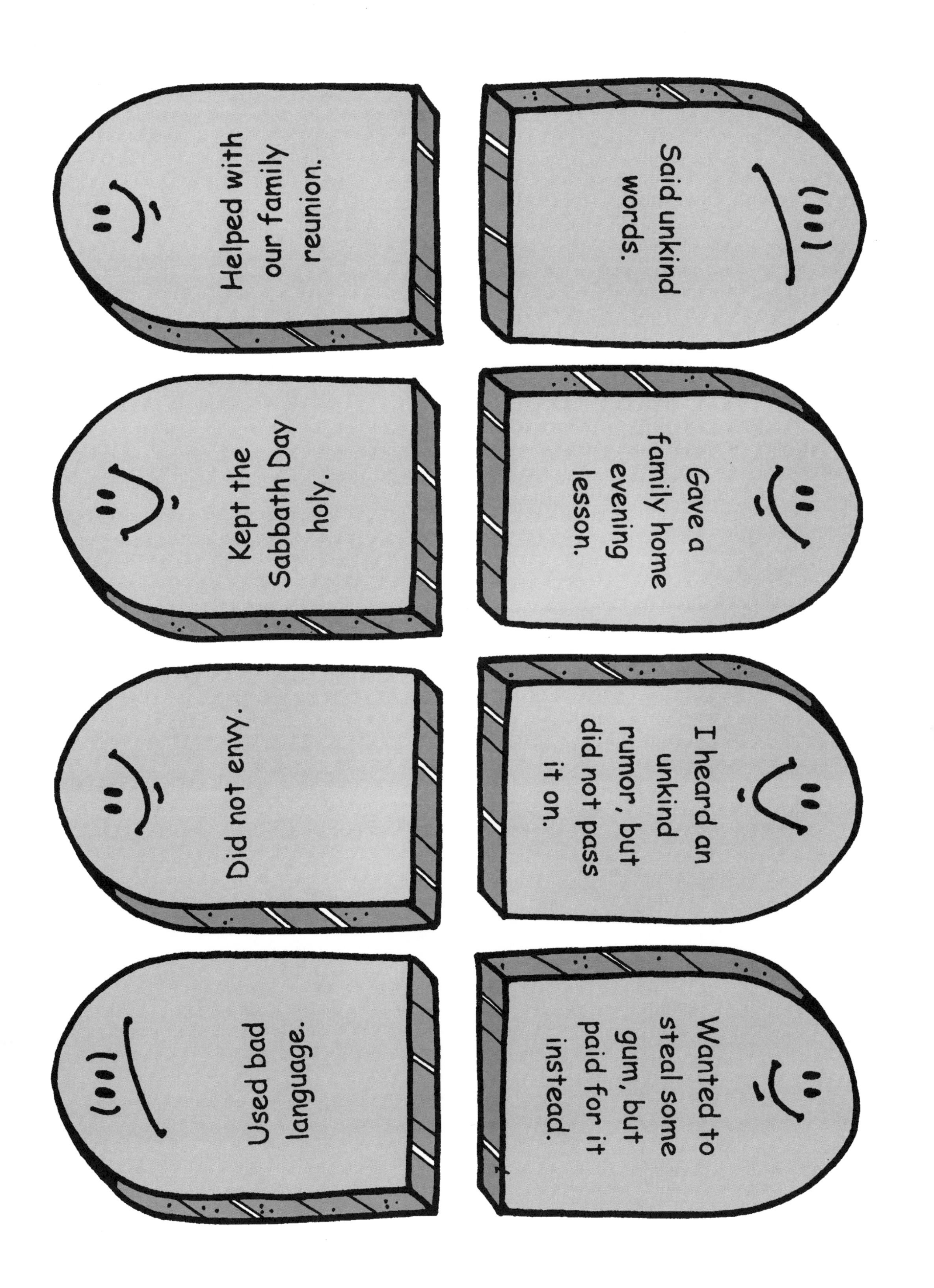

Helped with our family reunion.
Said unkind words.
Kept the Sabbath Day holy.
Gave a family home evening lesson.
Did not envy.
I heard an unkind rumor, but did not pass it on.
Used bad language.
Wanted to steal some gum, but paid for it instead.

#4 – Faith: FAITH: My Faith Can Grow

Scripture to Memorize: Memorize the Alma 32:21 scripture (shown right) on page 53.

BITE SIZE MEMORIZE

If ye have faith ye p 4 things which R n, which R true. Alma 32:21

Lesson Ideas:

QUESTIONS: Ask the following questions and talk about faith.

#1: What does it mean to have faith? (To believe and trust that something is real and true, even though we have not seen it.)

#2: What does it mean to have faith in the Lord Jesus Christ? (To trust that he lives and loves us, that he is Heavenly Father's son.)

#3: How can our faith in Jesus Christ grow? (By praying, reading the scriptures, hearing the word of God from his servants, and keeping the commandments.)

STORIES:

• Show picture of Bartimaeus (#144 or 145) from the ward library. Bartimaeus the blind man sat on the side of the highway begging. When Jesus came near, Bartimaeus begged to be healed (Mark 10:46-52). Tell children he received his sight because of his faith in Jesus.

• Read Matthew 8:5-10, 13. The centurion asked Jesus to heal his servant. Ask children, "How can our faith be like the faith of the centurion?" (We can believe that Heavenly Father can heal those who are sick when they receive a priesthood blessing.)

ACTIVITY: My Faith Is Growing

(Choices: Strong and Wilting Plant Match Game)

OBJECTIVE: Help children make positive choices that help their faith grow.

TO MAKE:

1. Cut out and mount the weak plant and the strong plant parts A and B (pages 55-62) on two separate posters and laminate.
2. Mount the leaves (pages 63-70) on cardstock paper, laminate and cut out. Place leaves in a bag to draw from.
3. Mount the plant posters on the board.

TO PLAY:

1. Ask children to take turns drawing leaves from the bag.
2. Tell children the leaves are choices that will help their faith grow or stop it from growing.
3. Have children place the leaves on the growing plant or the wilting plant, e.g., the "I showed reverence" leaf should be placed on the growing plant.

THOUGHT TREAT (when appropriate): Strong Lettuce Salad. Give children a leaf of strong healthy lettuce and one that is wilted. Have them choose which one they want to eat to be strong. Say, "'Lettuce' help our faith grow strong by making good choices."

All images can be printed in color or black and white, using the *Gospel Fun Activities* CD-ROM.

BITE SIZE MEMORIZE

If ye have
faith ye + p
4 things
which R
+ n,
which R
true. Alma 32:21

↑ Cut carefully along the inside of the dotted line. ↑

Do not cut on the dotted line. Use this margin to mount the other side.

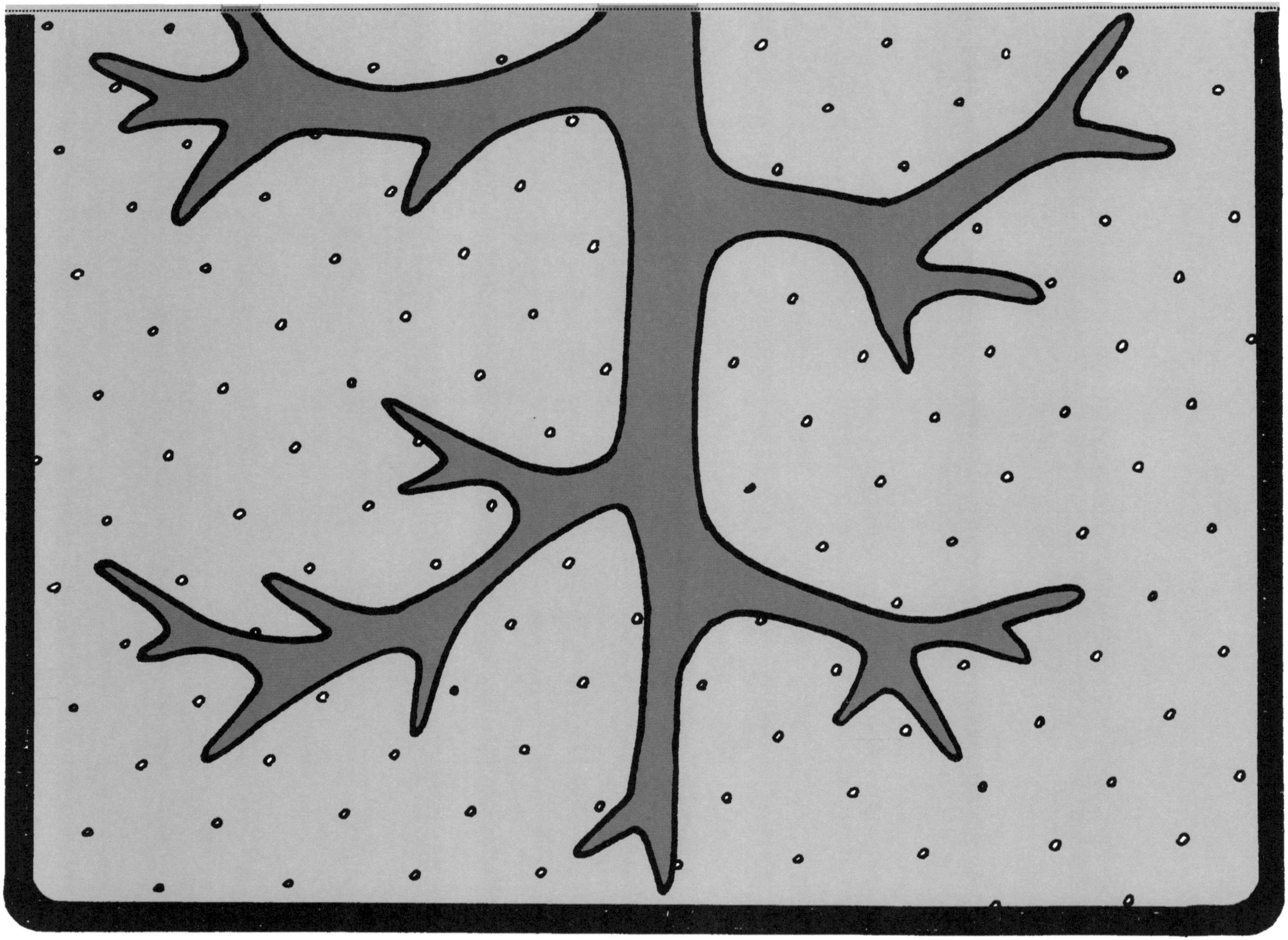

Cut carefully along the inside of the dotted line.

Do not cut on the dotted line. Use this margin to mount the other side.

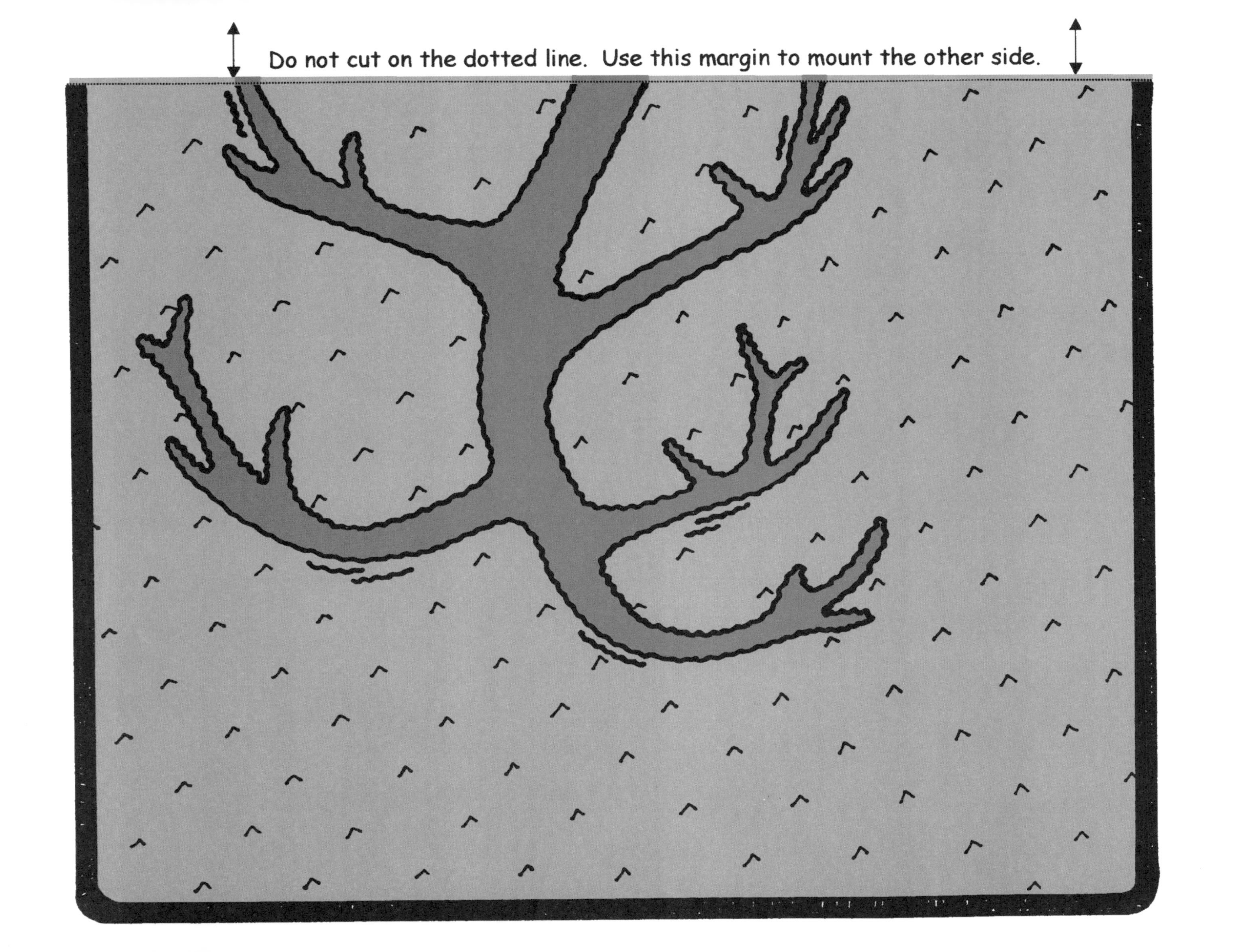

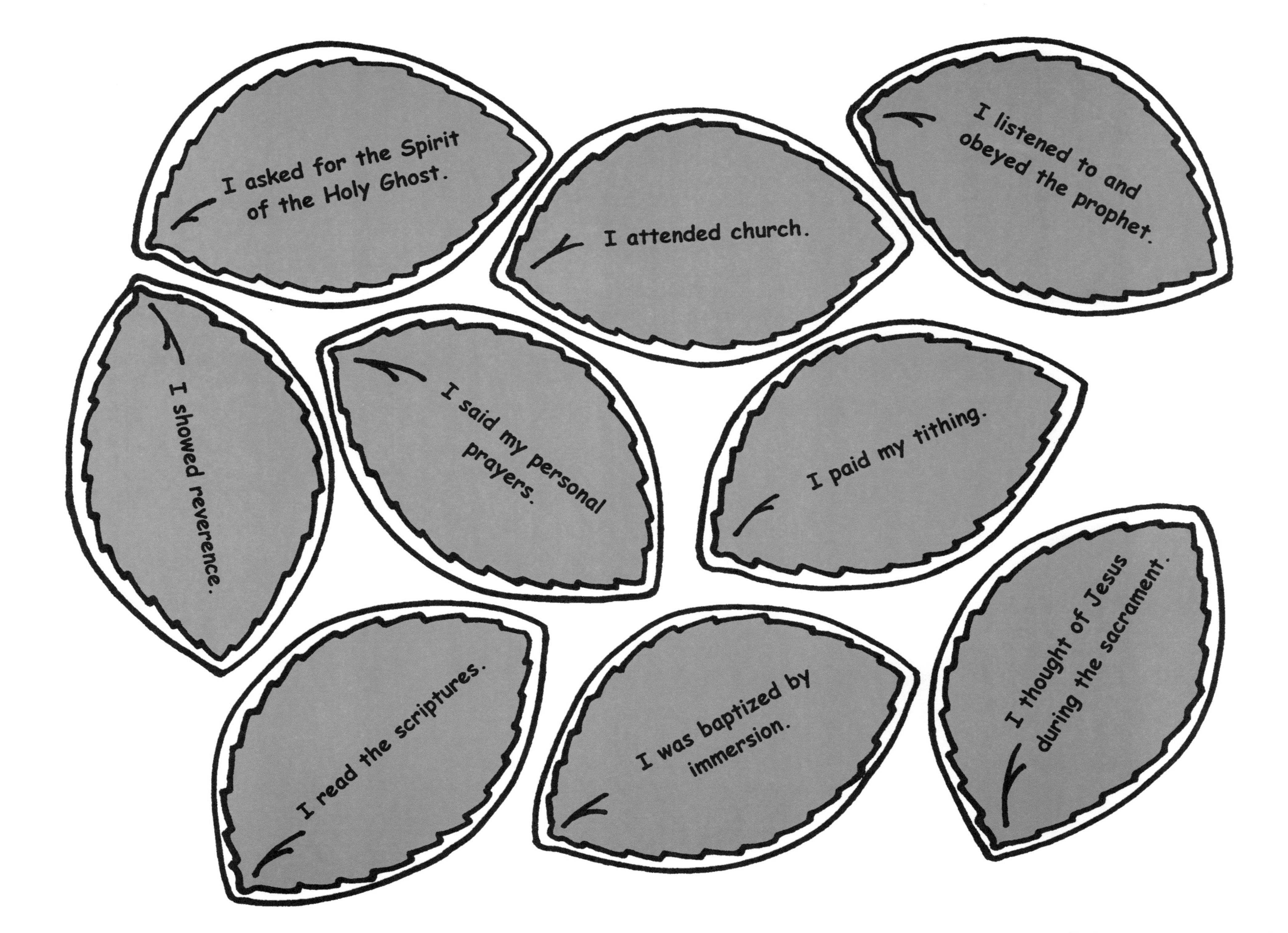

I asked for the Spirit of the Holy Ghost.
I attended church.
I listened to and obeyed the prophet.
I showed reverence.
I said my personal prayers.
I paid my tithing.
I read the scriptures.
I was baptized by immersion.
I thought of Jesus during the sacrament.

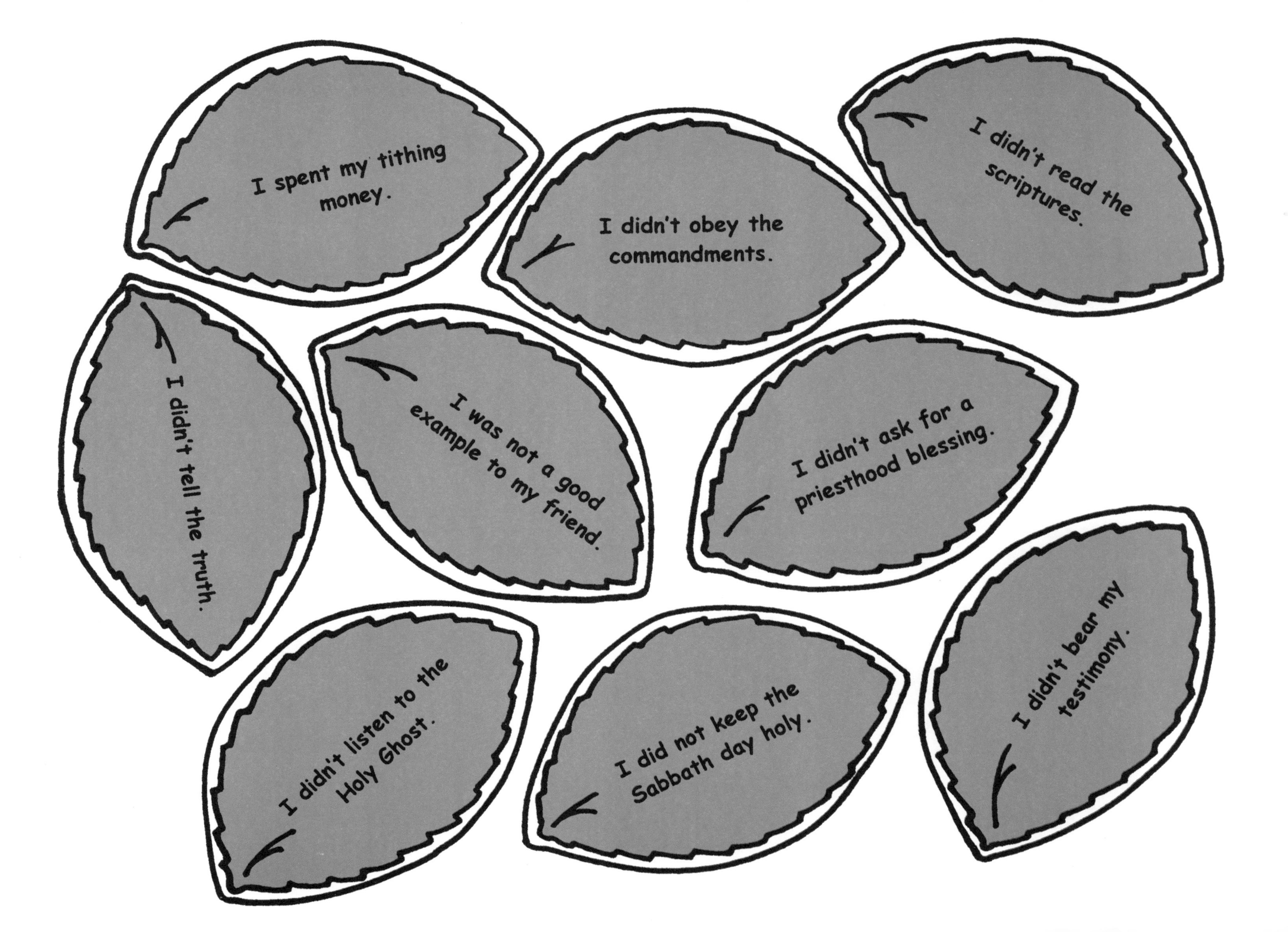
I spent my tithing money.
I didn't obey the commandments.
I didn't read the scriptures.
I didn't tell the truth.
I was not a good example to my friend.
I didn't ask for a priesthood blessing.
I didn't listen to the Holy Ghost.
I did not keep the Sabbath day holy.
I didn't bear my testimony.

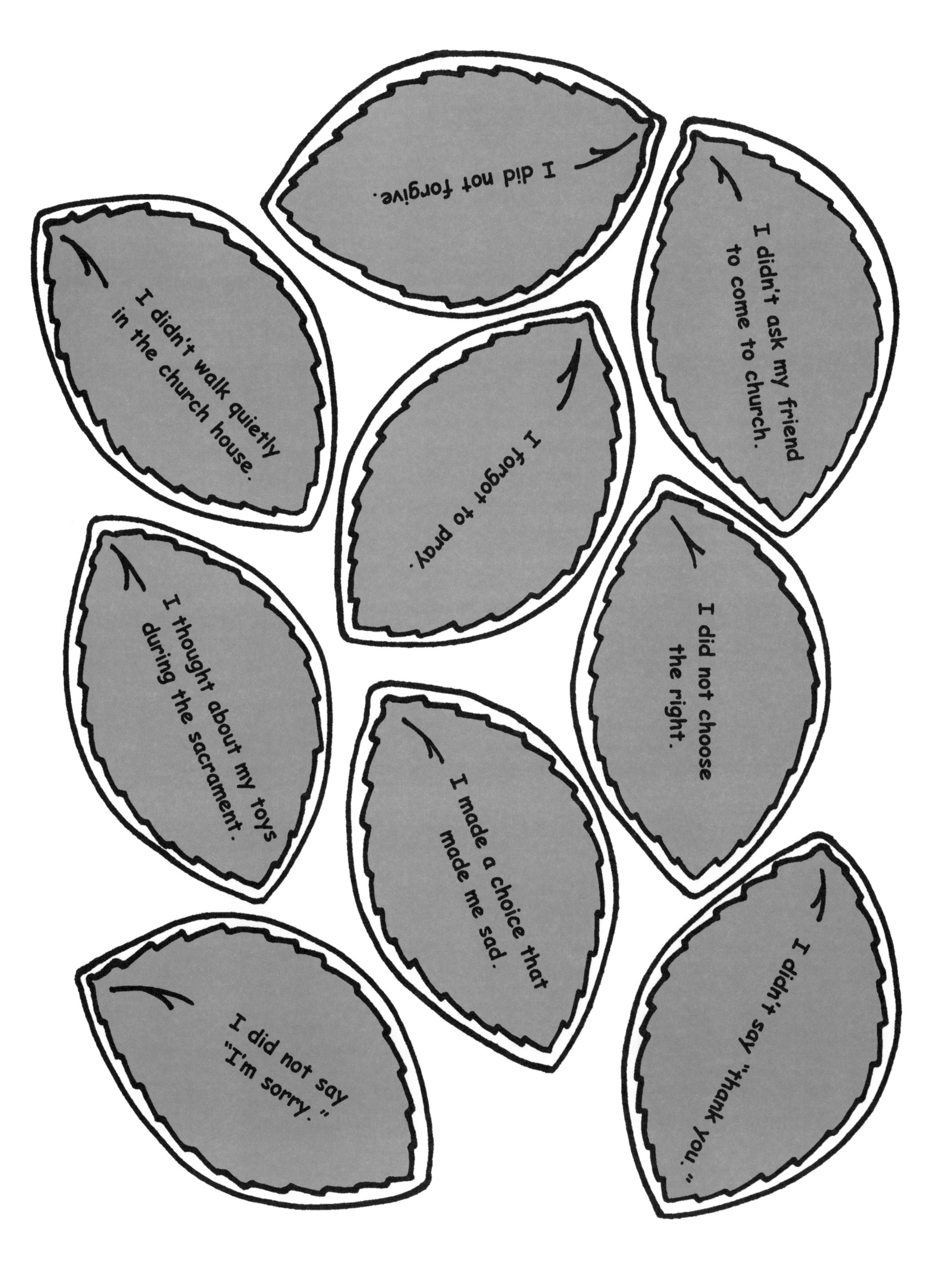
I did not forgive.
I didn't walk quietly in the church house.
I didn't ask my friend to come to church.
I forgot to pray.
I thought about my toys during the sacrament.
I did not choose the right.
I made a choice that made me sad.
I did not say "I'm sorry."
I didn't say "thank you."

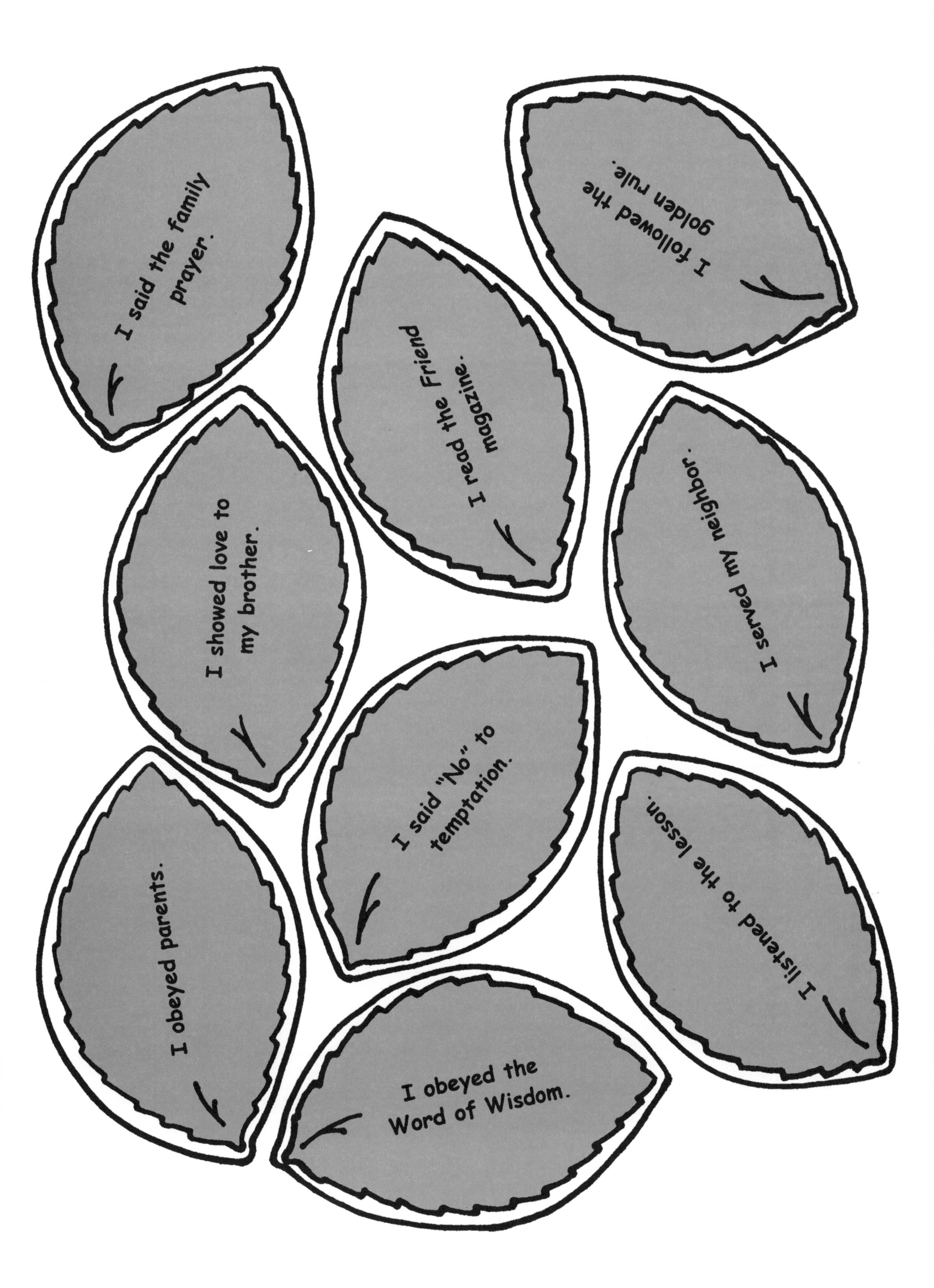

I said the family prayer.
I followed the golden rule.
I read the Friend magazine.
I showed love to my brother.
I served my neighbor.
I said "No" to temptation.
I obeyed parents.
I listened to the lesson.
I obeyed the Word of Wisdom.

#5 – Follow Jesus: I Will Always Remember Jesus

Scripture to Memorize: Memorize the Mosiah 18:10 scripture (shown right) on page 73.

Lesson Ideas:

PICTURE: Obtain picture of Jesus and a child being baptized.

QUESTION: Ask "What do we promise Heavenly Father when we are baptized?" and answer the question using the scriptures, Primary lessons, and other sources (below) to teach.

#1: We take upon us the name of Jesus Christ and are called His sons and daughters (2 Nephi 31:13-17; Mosiah 5:7-15; Alma 46:15; and *Primary 4—Book of Mormon*, lesson 12 enrichment activity 3).

#2: We promise we will always remember Jesus (3 Nephi 18:7-12; Doctrine and Covenants 20:77, 79; *Primary 3—CTR B*, lesson 32; *Primary Video Collection*, "Baptism").

#3: We promise we will keep His commandments (John 14:15; Mosiah 2:22; *Primary 3—CTR B*, lesson 3; *Primary 4—Book of Mormon*, lesson 15).

(Find the Light Situation Spotlight)

OBJECTIVE: Help children follow the light or example of Jesus Christ.

TO MAKE:

1. Mount Jesus picture and lightbulbs (pages (75-82) on cardstock paper, laminate, and cut out.
2. Tape the picture of Jesus in the center of the board or wall. Tape lightbulbs around the room.

INTRODUCE ACTIVITY:

1. Tell children that if we always remember Jesus and keep his commandments he will give us light. In 3 Nephi 18:7 and D&C 20:77, 79, we are promised that if we follow Jesus he will give us his Spirit to be with us. His Spirit is a light that guides us in the choices we make.
2. If we always remember Jesus we will follow his light, we will follow his example and live as he would live. When a situation is placed before you, do you follow the light?
3. *"Jesus* [spake] *again unto them, saying, I am the light of the world: he that followeth me shall not walk in darkness, but shall have the light of life"* (John 8:12). We don't have to walk in darkness. Each day we can find the light as we choose the right and follow Jesus.

ACTIVITY:

1. Choose a child to find a lightbulb mounted on the wall and come to the front of the room.
2. Have the child read the situation and ask, "What would Jesus do to find the light?" Discuss with the children the right action for the situation.
3. Children then can place the lightbulb on the board or wall around the picture of Jesus.

THOUGHT TREAT (when appropriate): Lightbulb Cookie: Shape and decorate a cookie like a light bulb. Frost the top with yellow frosting and the bottom with chocolate (lines). Decorate a smile face with chocolate frosting from a tube. As you eat, tell children they can light up their life each day as they remember Jesus and follow his light.

 All images can be printed in color or black and white, using the *Gospel Fun Activities* CD-ROM.

BITE SIZE MEMORIZE
[+ ing] ye
have N+tered
N2 a coven+
with [ ], t+
Christ
ye serve him
and +p his ,
t+ he may
out his +it
more a+ +d+ +ly
upon U.
Mosiah 18:10

Always Remember Jesus

Always remember Jesus...
When I come home from school the house is a mess and I don't feel like helping, so I...
Always remember Jesus...
My brother always forgets to make his bed and pick up his room, so I...
Always remember Jesus...
Some kids at school like to swear, so I...
Always remember Jesus...
My friend in Primary said he would bear his testimony if I would, but I'm afraid to, so I ...
Always remember Jesus...
After Primary class the kids were running down the hall and they asked me to come, so I ...
Always remember Jesus...
We sit on the back row in Primary and when the talks are given, my friend talks to me, so I...
Always remember Jesus...
My friend at school will write down the answers and pass them to me during a test, so I...
Always remember Jesus...
I really wanted a cool pair of ski gloves but didn't have any money, so I...

Always remember Jesus...
My parents don't attend church, so I...
Always remember Jesus...
A boy in my Primary class likes to kick me during Sharing Time, so I...
Always remember Jesus...
When it comes to singing time, I don't think I sing good, so I...
Always remember Jesus...
I found some money on the floor in the dressing room, so I...
Always remember Jesus...
My friend gave me some money and asked me to pay it to the teacher for his school lunch. so I...
Always remember Jesus...
My friends say it's not cool to say hi and wave to everyone, just those we like, so I...
Always remember Jesus...
My neighbor's wife is out on a cold day shoveling snow, so I...
Always remember Jesus...
The woman next door works in her house and doesn't have time to play with her children, so I...

Always remember Jesus…
I earned some money and wanted to spend it all, so I…
Always remember Jesus…
My brother broke my favorite toy, so I…
Always remember Jesus…
No one smiled at me in Primary today, so I…
Always remember Jesus…
My sister wanted to play with me when my friends were over, so I…
Always remember Jesus…
Friends were saying bad things about a girl at school, so I…
Always remember Jesus…
My mother asked me to help with the dishes when my friend came over, so I…
Always remember Jesus…
My school teacher told me that I shouldn't come in late, so I…
Always remember Jesus…
I took something that didn't belong to be but my friends didn't see, so I…

#6 – Holy Ghost: The Holy Ghost Will Help Me Choose the Right

Scripture to Memorize: Memorize the 2 Nephi 32:5 scripture (shown right) on page 85.

Lesson Ideas:

QUESTION: Ask "How will the Holy Ghost help us keep our baptismal covenant?" and answer the question using the following:

#1: The Holy Ghost bears witness to us when we are taught the truth. The Holy Ghost testifies of Jesus Christ (John 15:26; 1 Corinthians 2:9-12; 12:3; *Gospel Principles*, chapter 7; *Primary 1*, lesson 7).

#2: The Holy Ghost will prompt, teach, and guide us (John 14:26; 16:13; 2 Nephi 32:5, *Primary 3*, lesson 26; *Primary 4*, lesson 40; *Primary 7*, lesson 36).

#3: We will listen to and obey the promptings of the Holy Ghost. The Holy Ghost will help us choose the right (Moroni 10:3-5; Doctrine and Covenants 8:2; 9:7-9; *Primary 3*, lesson 12 enrichment activity 4; *Primary 5*, lesson 7, enrichment activities; *Primary 7*, lesson 36).

ACTIVITY: The Holy Ghost Will Help Me Choose the Right

(Trail to Holy Ghost Town Game)

OBJECTIVE: Help children know that through choosing the right, the Holy Ghost will be a part of their life to prompt, teach, and guide them.

TO MAKE: Mount the following images (pages 87-103) on cardstock paper, laminate and cut out Death Valley, Dynamite/Start, and Holy Ghost Town signs, Trail Stones, Boot Markers, and Trail Mix cards. (You'll need a die as well.)

TO SET UP:

1. Tape the Death Valley sign on the bottom and Holy Ghost Town at the top of the board.
2. Tape the rock signs making a trail to and from the two signs.
3. Tape the Start sign on the trail as shown.

TO PLAY: Tell children, "We are going to play a game called Trail to Holy Ghost Town. Let's imagine we are going to a special town filled with good people who choose the right. They listen to the promptings of the Holy Ghost, which makes this town a happy town. Let's imagine that those who do wrong actions and do not repent of these actions go to Death Valley, a place where the Holy Ghost cannot dwell. The first team to get to Holy Ghost Town wins the game!"

1. Divide children into two teams and give each team a Boot marker to place on the Dynamite/Start position on the board. Use double-stick tape to keep marker on the board.
2. Flip a coin to determine which team goes first.
3. Teams take turns rolling a die and moving that number of rocks along the trail, following "move forward" or "move backward" signs on rocks.
4. When players land on a Trail Mix rock, draw a situation from the Trail Mix container, read the situation, and move forward or backward as indicated on the card. Double-stick tape the card to the board. *Note:* If the situation on the Trail Mix card tells you to go back, have the child tell how he or she could change the action on the card, choosing the right, so they can have the Holy Ghost guide them.
5. If you land on Death Valley, roll the die on your next turn to get back on the trail.
6. The first team or player to get to Holy Ghost Town wins!

THOUGHT TREAT (when appropriate): Trail Treats (rock-shaped candy). Give each child one or two brown jelly beans that resemble the rock on the trail. As they eat, ask them to name a step they should take to keep the Holy Ghost with them, e.g., pray, keep the commandments, read the scriptures, be kind.

 All images can be printed in color or black and white, using the *Gospel Fun Activities* CD-ROM.

BITE SIZE MEMORIZE

If ye N+ter in by the way, and receive the Holy Ghost, it Show N2 U all things what ye should do.

2 Nephi 32:5

Death Valley

STORE
LIVERY
Holy Ghost Town

MOVE BACK 3
MOVE BACK 1
MOVE AHEAD 1
MOVE AHEAD 1
MOVE BACK 4
MOVE BACK 2
MOVE BACK 1
MOVE BACK 3
START

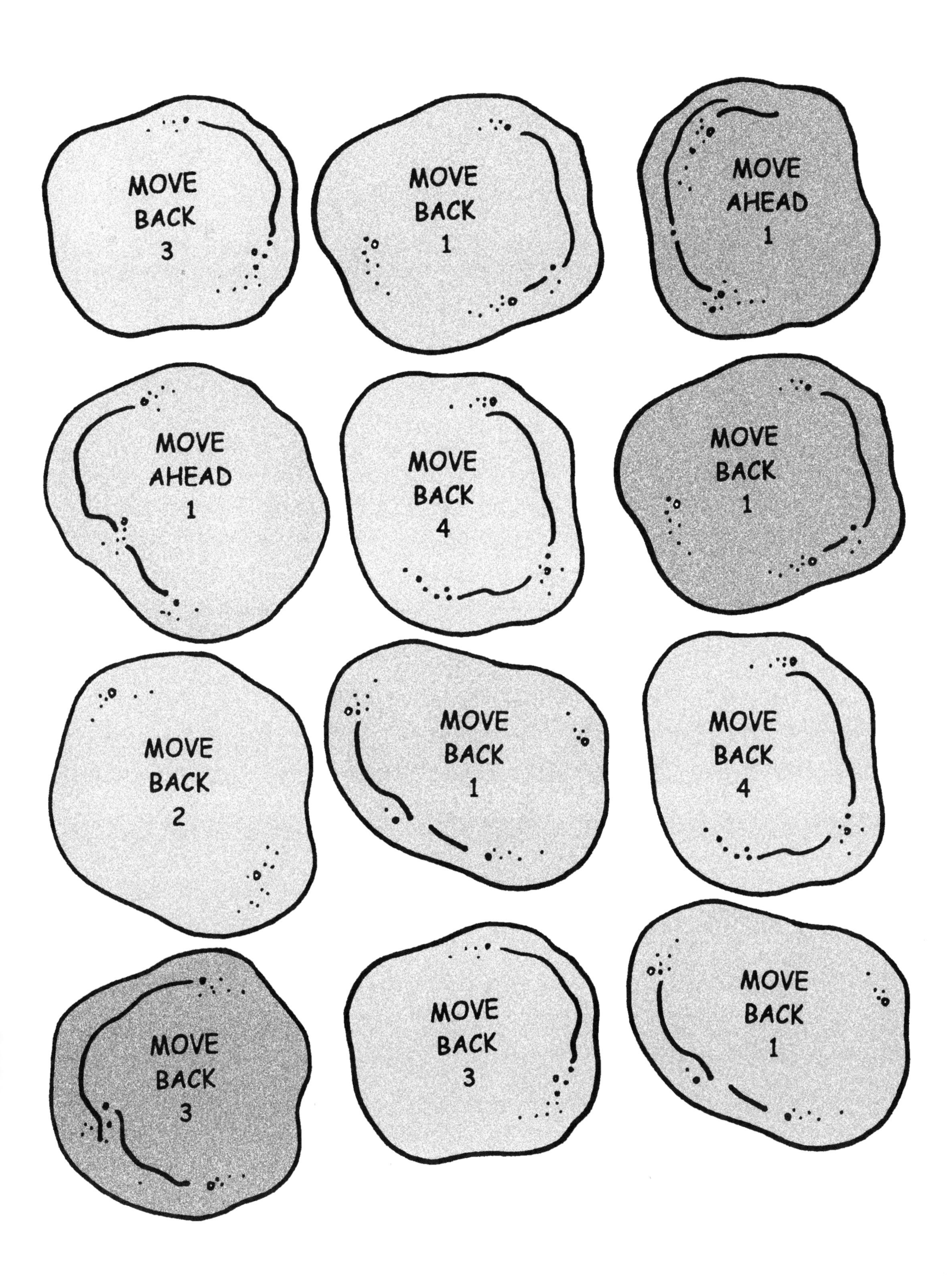
MOVE BACK 3
MOVE BACK 1
MOVE AHEAD 1
MOVE AHEAD 1
MOVE BACK 4
MOVE BACK 1
MOVE BACK 2
MOVE BACK 1
MOVE BACK 4
MOVE BACK 3
MOVE BACK 3
MOVE BACK 1

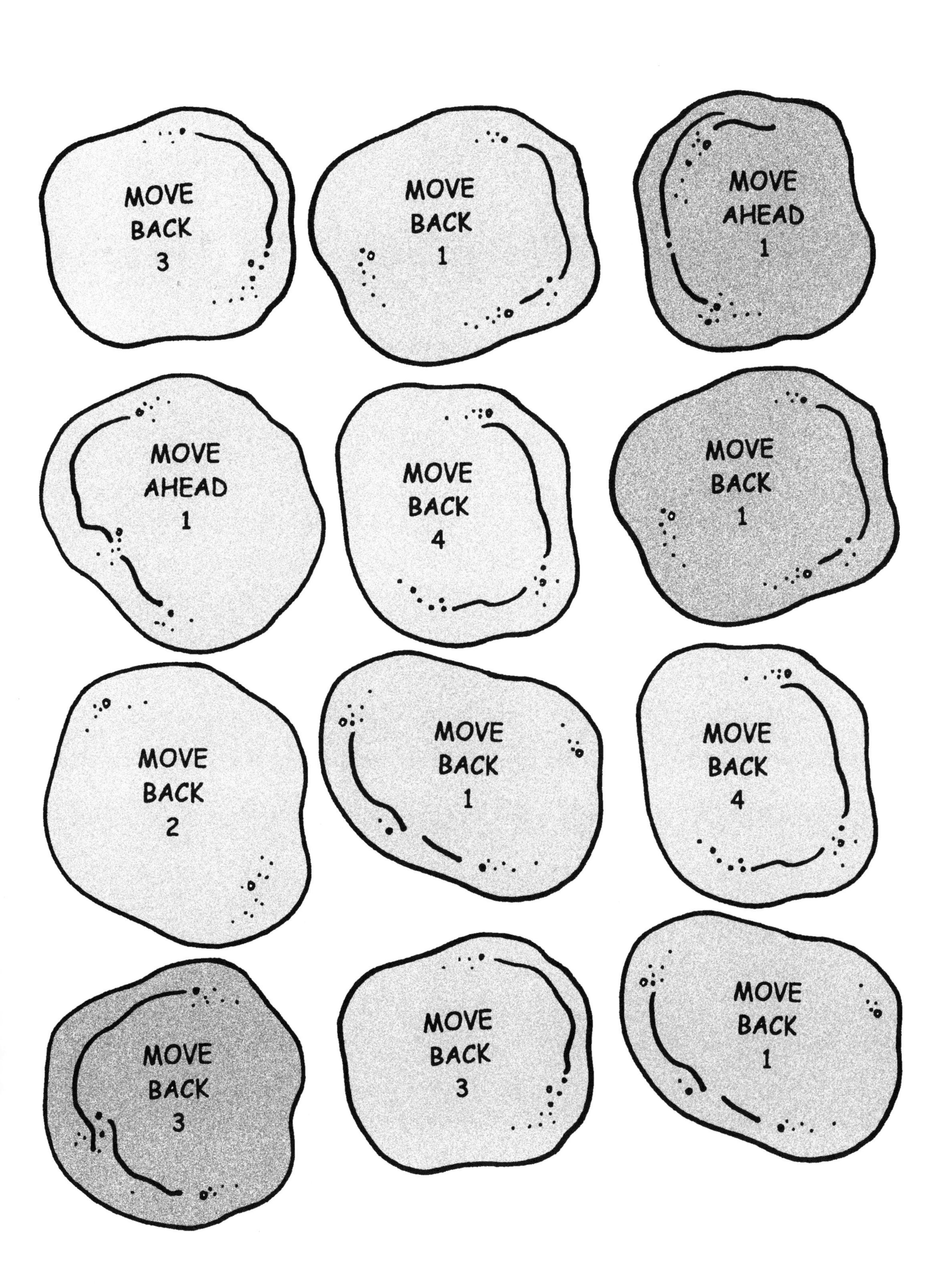
MOVE BACK 3
MOVE BACK 1
MOVE AHEAD 1
MOVE AHEAD 1
MOVE BACK 4
MOVE BACK 1
MOVE BACK 2
MOVE BACK 1
MOVE BACK 4
MOVE BACK 3
MOVE BACK 3
MOVE BACK 1

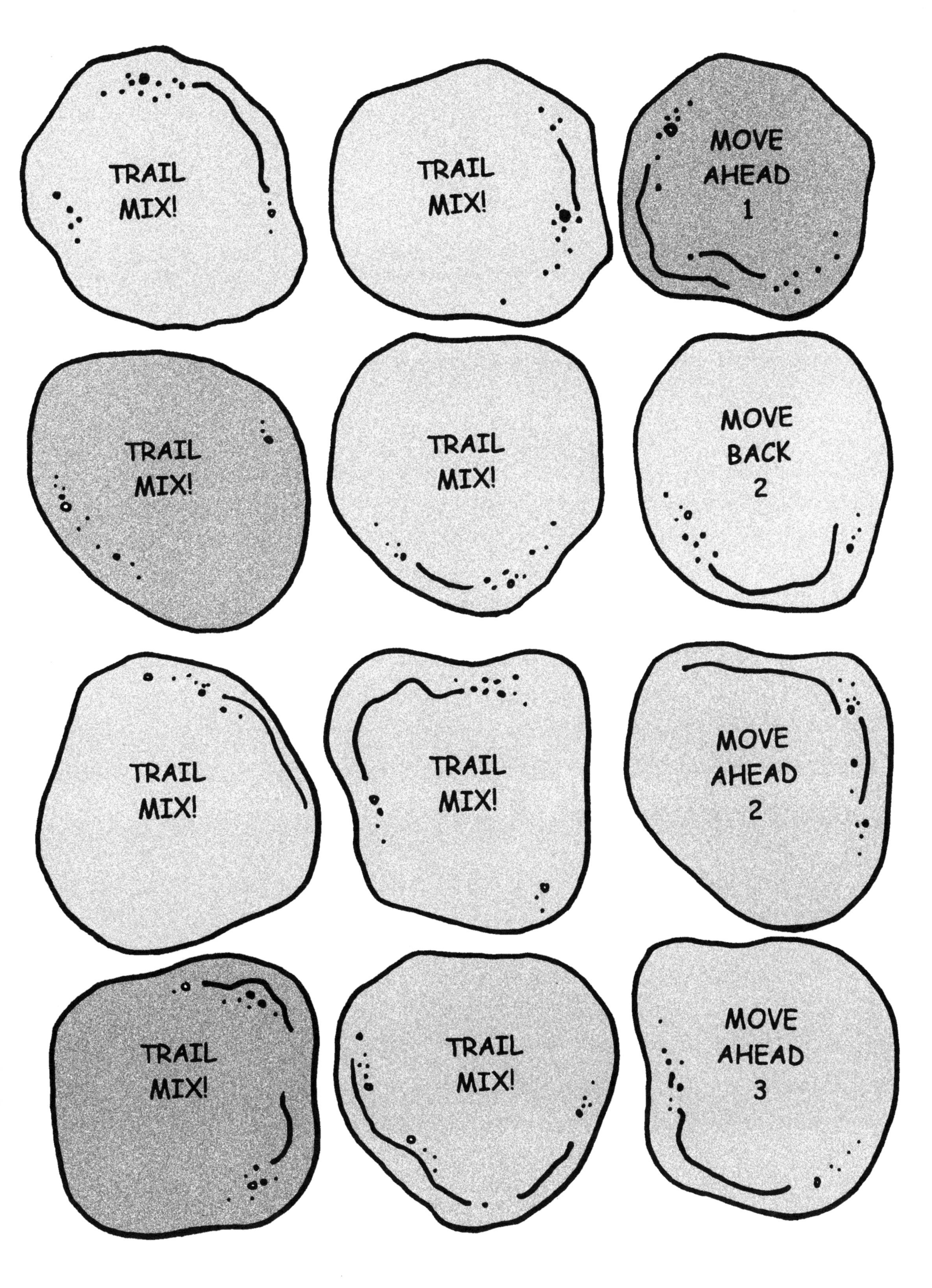

TRAIL MIX!
TRAIL MIX!
MOVE AHEAD 1
TRAIL MIX!
TRAIL MIX!
MOVE BACK 2
TRAIL MIX!
TRAIL MIX!
MOVE AHEAD 2
TRAIL MIX!
TRAIL MIX!
MOVE AHEAD 3

You say your prayers morning and night to keep heaven in sight (move ahead 1).
You pray and ask Heavenly Father to help you stay on the strait and narrow path (move ahead 1).
It's time to get ready for church but you tell your parents you are sick when you are just tired (move back 2).
Your parents ask you to feed your baby brother but you feed yourself first (move back 1).
You tell your teacher you read your assignment when you forgot (move back 1).
You read the scriptures each day and learn about the gospel of Jesus Christ (move ahead 2).
You take turns on the playground and give the other children a chance to play (move ahead 1).
You want a bike like your friend's so you beg your Mom to buy one when you have no money (move back 1).

You say excuse me, thank you and please (move ahead 1).
It is not Thanksgiving but you thank Heavenly Father anyway (move ahead 1).
You are in a hurry to get to school and you don't stop to help a boy who fell off his bike (move back 1).
Your mother asks you to take a get well card to a neighbor on your way to play, but you forget (move back 1).
You are asked to rake the leaves and help with the garden but you ride your bike instead (move back 1).
You kick the dog when she gets in your way (move back 2).
You tell your sister she did a good job (move ahead 1).
Your mother asks you to wear your coat and you leave it home (move back 1).

You like to jump on the trampoline and share it with your friends (move ahead 1).
You felt like yelling at your brother when he yelled at you, but you didn't (move ahead 2).
You like to throw rocks at cats, dogs, and birds (move back 2).
It's your turn at the drinking fountain but you let a smaller child in front of you (move ahead 1).
Your friends want you to take some candy at the store without paying, but you said, "no" (move ahead 1).
You are at a friend's party and decide to take one of his birthday presents home (move back 2).
You work hard to get your homework done so you don't have to do school work on Sunday (move ahead 1).
You are tempted to smoke a cigarette but you don't (move ahead 2).

You take tithing money and spend it on a new bike (move back 1).

You are leaving with your family for a few days and you forget to put extra food out for the dog (move back 2).

You raise your hand to answer questions in Primary class (move ahead 1).

You play with a nonmember friend but don't invite him to the Primary activity (move back 1).

You are nice to your sister when Mom is around, but when she's gone you are unkind (move back 1).

You read a Book of Mormon story to a friend (move ahead 1).

You want to give a talk in Primary but never raise your hand (move back 1).

You are asked to help lead the younger Primary children in a game and you say "yes" (move ahead 1).

#7 – Missionary Talents:

I Will Share the Gospel with Others

Scripture to Memorize: Memorize the Matthew 5:16 scripture (shown right) on page 107.

Lesson Ideas:

QUESTION: Ask "What other special helps has Heavenly Father given us to help us keep our baptismal covenant?" and answer the question using the scriptures, Primary lessons, or other references (below) to teach.

#1: We can obey His commandments and follow the counsel of His living prophet (1 John 2:3; Doctrine and Covenants 1:38; current *Ensign* or conference issue).

#2: We can honor the priesthood (Hebrews 5:4; priesthood lessons *Primary 4,* lesson 30 and 31, *Primary 5,* lesson 8 and 26; *Primary 6,* lesson 19 and 33; *Primary 7,* lesson 15; *Gospel Principles* chapter 13).

#3: We can share the gospel with others (Luke 22:32; Doctrine and Covenants 4; *Primary 3,* lesson 25; *Primary 5,* lesson 29).

OBJECTIVE: Help children learn 10 ways they can soar high to stretch their talents as a missionary.

TO MAKE: Mount kites and kite tales (pages 109-122) on cardstock paper, laminate and cut out.
Note: To keep answer hidden, cut out answer (e.g., Read the Scriptures) and glue on the back of each kite. Place kite tail wordstrips in a container to draw from.
Obtain 10 twelve-inch pieces of string (or draw a string line on the blackboard beneath kites placed on the board).

ACTIVITY (For Junior Primary, cut activity in half, using only five kites):
1. Tell children, "Let's learn how we can soar high as missionaries." (Place kites on the board with double-stick tape and a string below each or draw a string on board).
2. Have children take turns coming up and drawing a missionary clue (found on the kite tail wordstrips). Read the clue and place the clue on the kite string that matches the number on the kite, e.g., place the clue with #1 on it below #1 kite.
3. Once three clues are placed on a string children try to guess what the missionary kite says. If the children guess correctly, turn the kite over to show them the answer. Review the three clues again.

TO MAKE ACTIVITY COMPETITIVE: Divide children into two teams. Tell children if they guess what the kite says before all the clues are read they earn 10 points for their team. The team with the most points wins after all kites are turned over. Attach the remaining clue(s) to the string to review.

FOLLOW-UP ACTIVITIES: Have children participate in these 10 activities by reciting the Articles of Faith, sharing their favorite scriptures, reading a story from *The Friend*, sharing their testimony of Jesus, showing a Church video, having a Primary activity and encouraging them to bring their nonmember friends, etc.

THOUGHT TREAT (when appropriate): Kite Cut-outs. Cut out kite shapes using fruit roll-ups or sugar cookie dough. Punch a hole and attach a licorice string. Bake cookies with licorice tied on or tie on after baked. Kite cookies can be painted using cookie paints (2 teaspoons milk and 2 drops of food coloring). Paint with a paint brush before baking, to decorate cookies. Tell children that they can soar high as a missionary if they keep their baptismal covenants.

 All images can be printed in color or black and white, using the *Gospel Fun Activities* CD-ROM.

BITE SIZE MEMORIZE
Let UR so
Shine B4 ,
t+ they may
UR good
works, and
glorify UR
Father which
is in .
Matt. 5:16

1. Learn the Articles of Faith
2. Read the scriptures

3
3. Be a friend
4
4. Read the Church magazines

6. Learn the Church hymns
5. Be courteous and kind

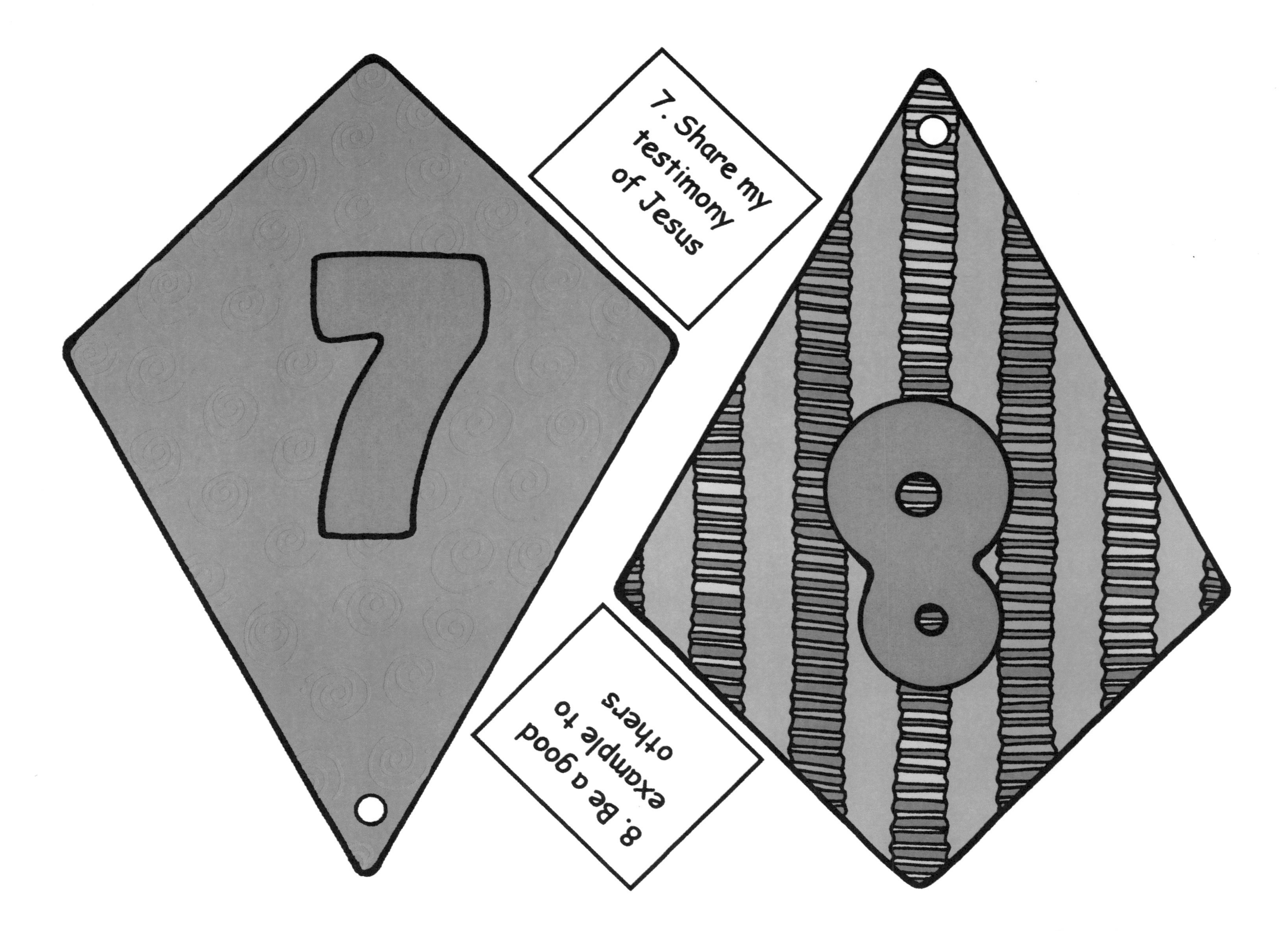
7
7. Share my testimony of Jesus
8
8. Be a good example to others

10. Invite friends to Church activities
9. Share a Church video with a friend

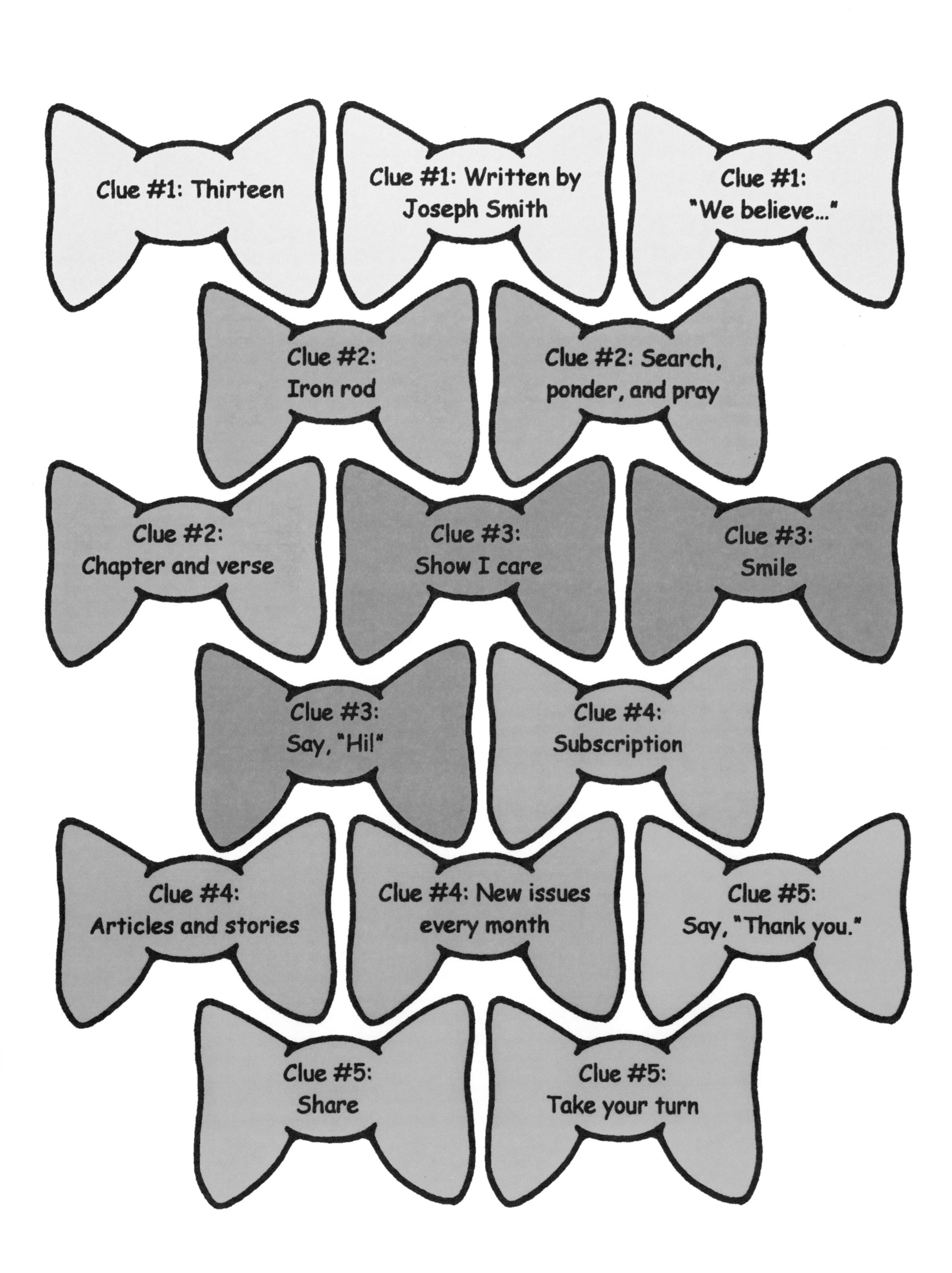

Clue #1: Thirteen
Clue #1: Written by Joseph Smith
Clue #1: "We believe…"
Clue #2: Iron rod
Clue #2: Search, ponder, and pray
Clue #2: Chapter and verse
Clue #3: Show I care
Clue #3: Smile
Clue #3: Say, "Hi!"
Clue #4: Subscription
Clue #4: Articles and stories
Clue #4: New issues every month
Clue #5: Say, "Thank you."
Clue #5: Share
Clue #5: Take your turn

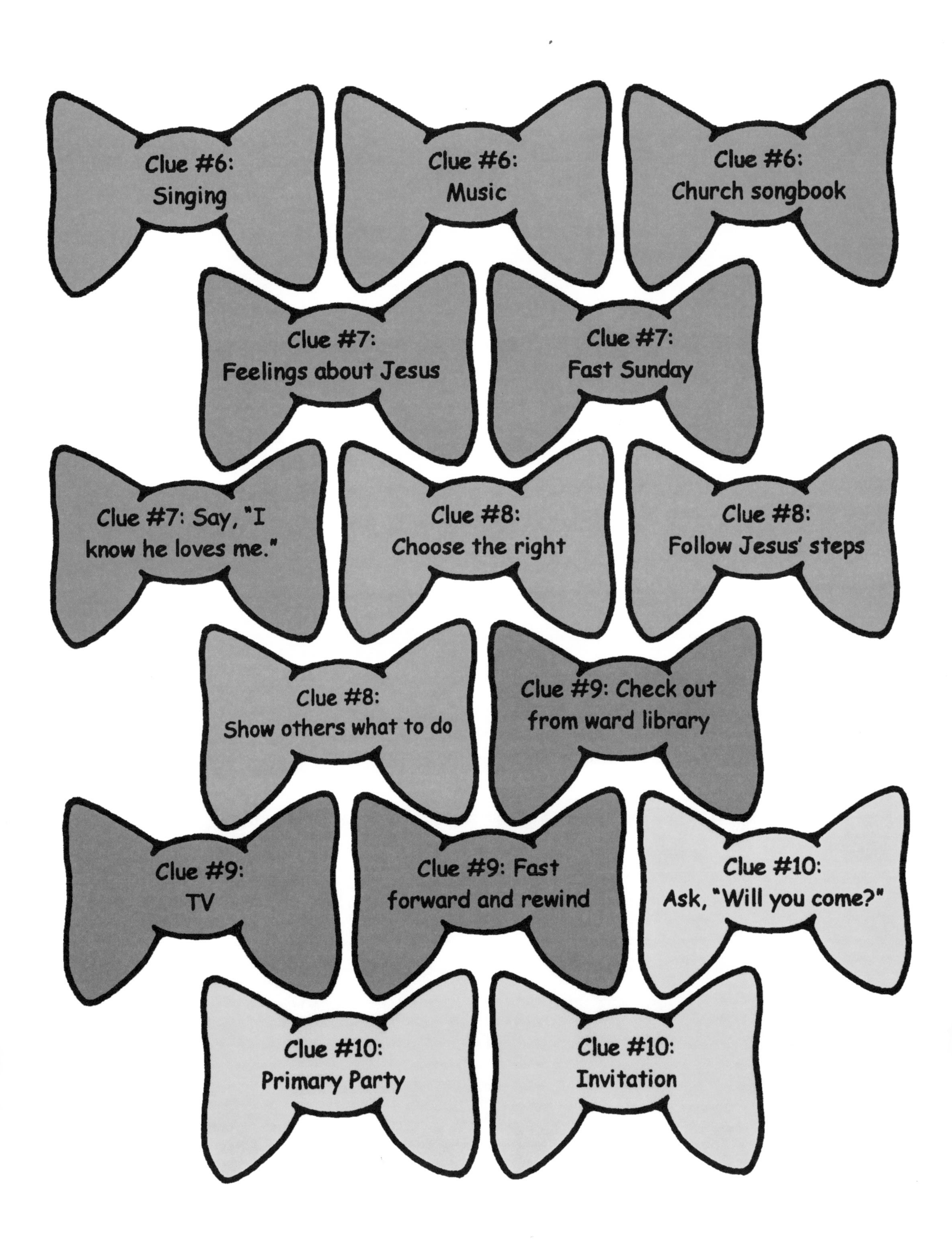
Clue #6:
Singing
Clue #6:
Music
Clue #6:
Church songbook
Clue #7:
Feelings about Jesus
Clue #7:
Fast Sunday
Clue #7: Say, "I know he loves me."
Clue #8:
Choose the right
Clue #8:
Follow Jesus' steps
Clue #8:
Show others what to do
Clue #9: Check out from ward library
Clue #9:
TV
Clue #9: Fast forward and rewind
Clue #10:
Ask, "Will you come?"
Clue #10:
Primary Party
Clue #10:
Invitation

#8 – Missionary Work: I Can Be a Fisher of Men, Like Jesus

Scripture to Memorize: Memorize the Matthew 4:19 scripture (shown right) on page 125.

Lesson Ideas:

QUESTIONS: Ask children the following:

#1: What are some things we can do to be a missionary, to share the gospel with others?

#2: Are you being a good example to others by the way you live?

#3: Are you sharing your testimony with your friends?

#4: Are you inviting friends to come to Primary?

#5: Are you living worthy to serve a mission someday?

ACTIVITY: I Can Be a Fisher of Men, Like Jesus

(Missionary Fish-ionary Fish Find)

OBJECTIVE: Help children learn the right (good fish-ionary) actions and the stinky (wrong fish-ionary) ways to be a missionary. Children can learn positive ways to share the gospel as they go fish.

TO MAKE:

1. Mount the fish (pages 127-136) on cardstock paper, laminate, and cut out.
2. Create a fish pole with a dowel and a long string tied to the end with a paper clip tied to the fish end.
3. Create a fish pond with a tablecloth draped over two chairs or easels.
4. Tie two long strings on the left and right side of the board (so children can attach good missionary fish to string). Have double-stick tape available to help children stick fish to the board (fish line).
5. Place team #1's fish on left and team #2's fish on the right.

*All images can be printed in color or black and white, using the *Gospel Fun Activities* CD-ROM.

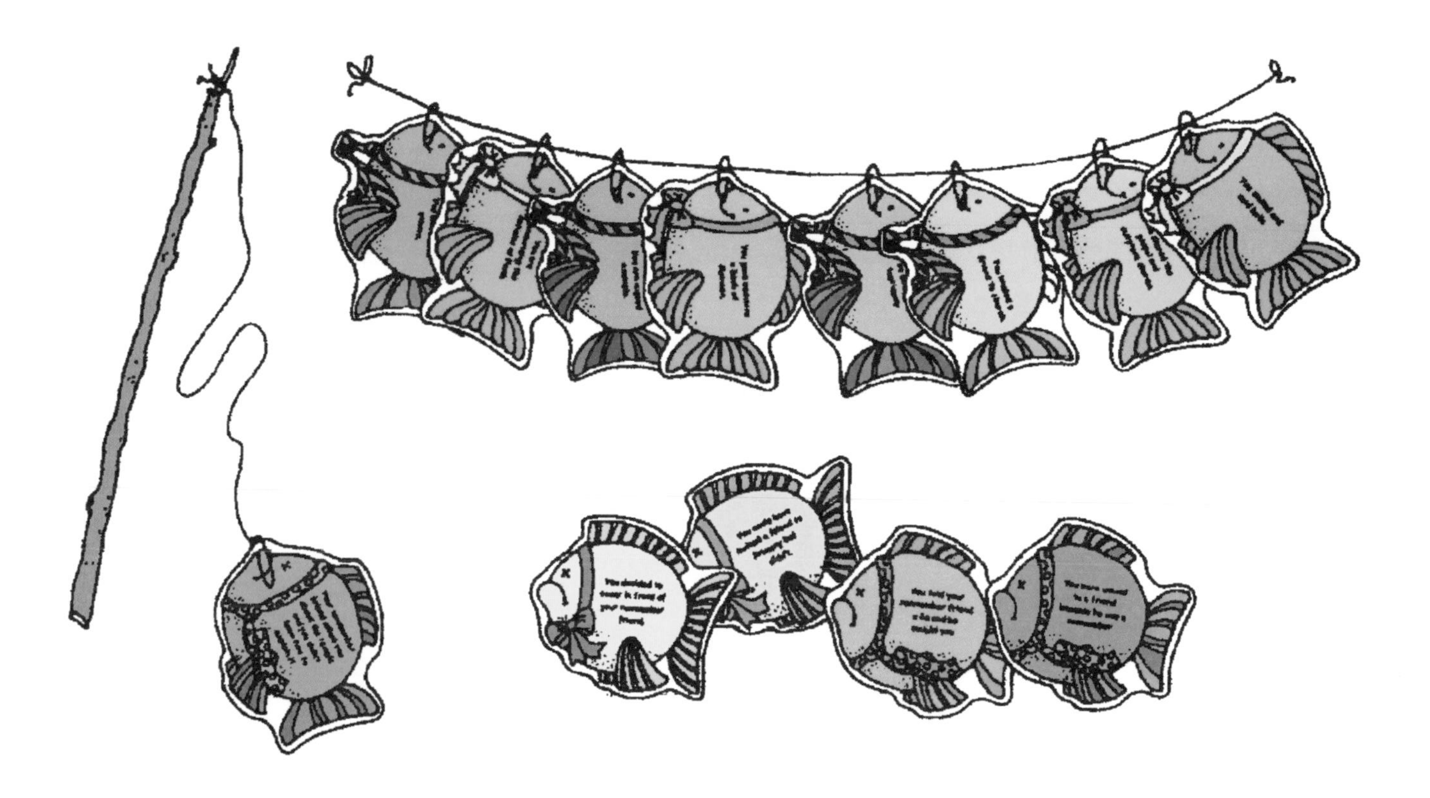

TO PLAY: Read Matthew 4:19-20 (fishers of men). Tell children, "We can become fishers of men like Jesus." He called his disciples to follow him, to teach the gospel. We too can follow Jesus and teach the gospel (to become fishers of men), and tell others about Jesus' church. Let's go fishing to find ways to be a good missionary fish-ionary and how to avoid being a stinky fish-ionary missionary.

1. Divide into two teams.
2. Take turns fishing (Primary leader paper clips a fish to pole string and yanks when fish is ready).
3. The child or leader reads fish aloud, and child decides if it is a good missionary or a stinky missionary action.
4. The child places the good fish on the board and the stinky fish on the table. The team with the most good fish-ionary fish win!

THOUGHT TREAT (when appropriate): Missionary Fish Wish Snacks, e.g., Goldfish crackers, gummy fish. Ask children as they fish their hands in to take a fish treat that they make a wish. Think of an action, something they can practice each day that will make them a better missionary, e.g., scripture reading, making friends, serving others.

PRIZE: Give each child a *I Can Be a Fisher of Men* card (pages 138-140). You will find eight colored cards and a set of eight black and white cards to cut out and use or copy. If you need more, print images from the *Gospel Fun Activities* CD-ROM*.

*All images can be printed in color or black and white, using the *Gospel Fun Activities* CD-ROM.

BITE SIZE MEMORIZE
And
Jesus
saith
N2 them,
Follow me,
and
make U
+
rs
of
.
Matt. 4:19

You are kind to your friends.
You paid tithing to build up the kingdom of God.
You told your friend a lie and he caught you.
You could have invited a friend to Primary but didn't.

You decided to
swear in front of
your friend.
You were unkind
to a friend because
he was a member
of another church.
You say "no" to
temptations.
You keep the
Word of Wisdom.

You told your friend you would play, and you forgot to call her.
Your friend asked you about the temple and you didn't know how to explain it.
You are memorizing the Articles of Faith.
You share with others.

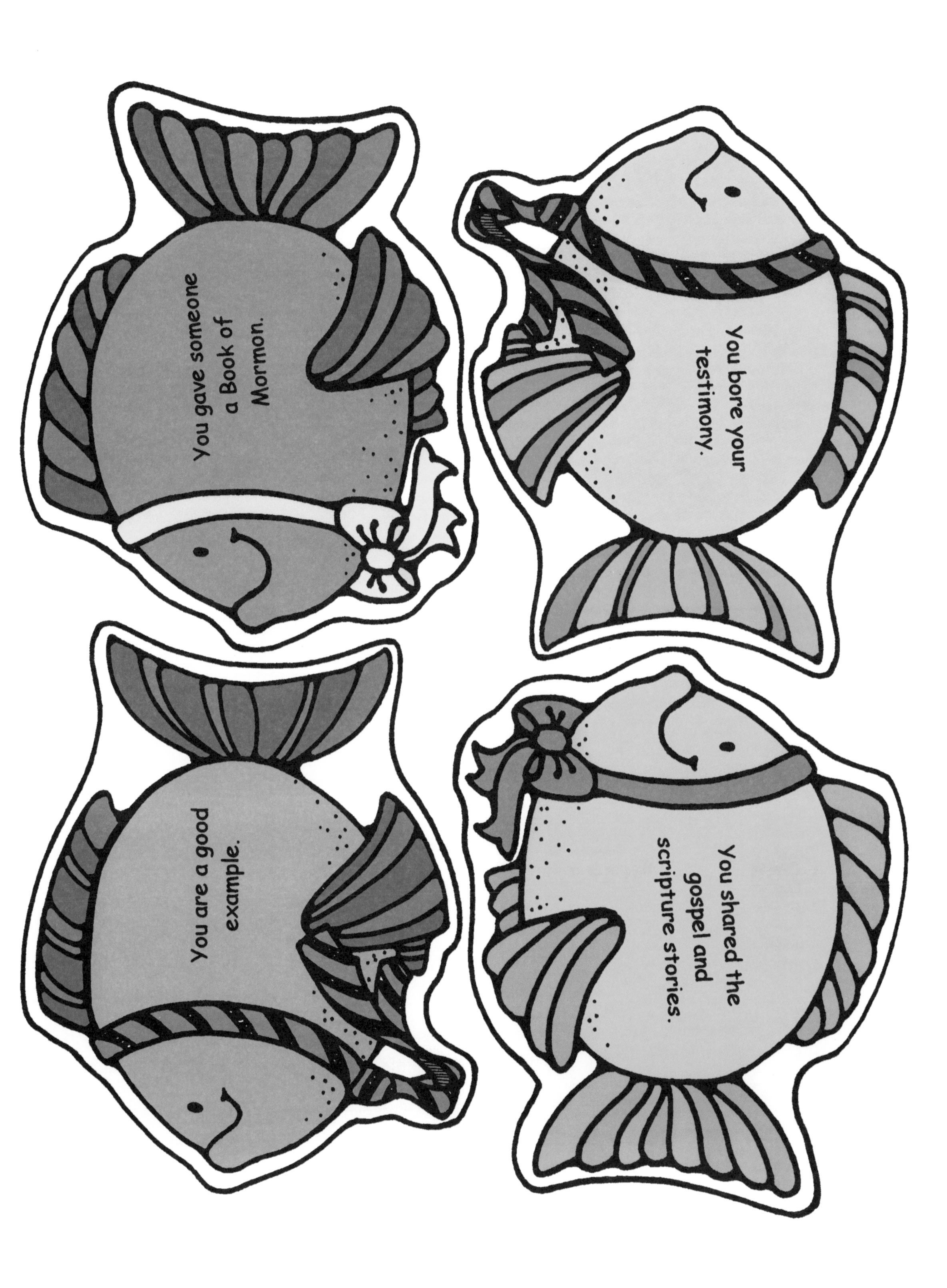
You gave someone a Book of Mormon.
You bore your testimony.
You are a good example.
You shared the gospel and scripture stories.

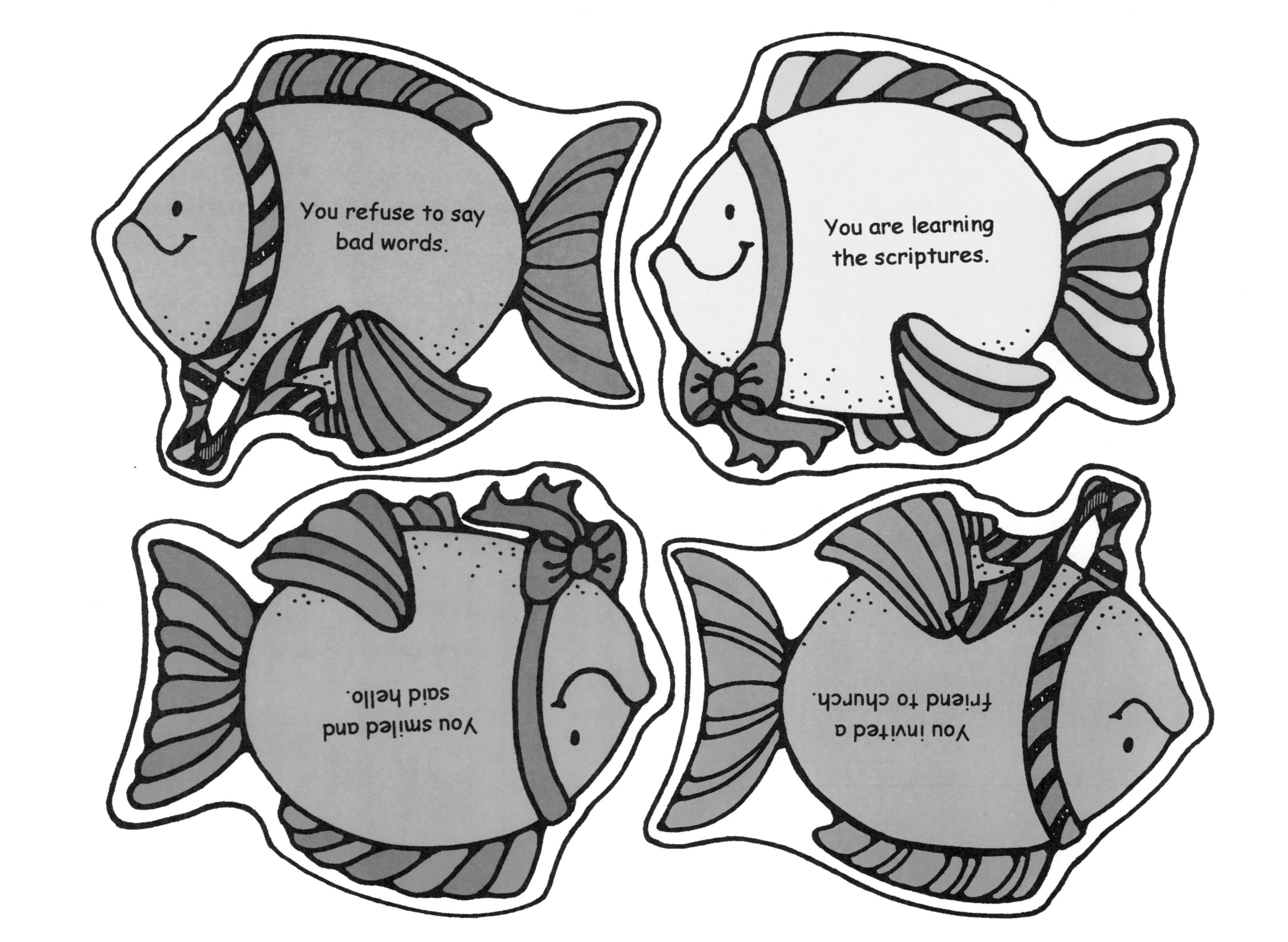
You refuse to say bad words.
You are learning the scriptures.
You smiled and said hello.
You invited a friend to church.

I can be a fisher of men

Name of Member "Fish"ionary

Name of Member "Fish"ionary

Name of Member "Fish"ionary

Name of Member "Fish"ionary

I can be a fisher of men.

Name of Member "Fish"ionary

Name of Member "Fish"ionary

I can be a fisher of men.

Name of Member "Fish"ionary

Name of Member "Fish"ionary

Name of Member "Fish"ionary

#9 – Repentance: Repentance Can Make Us Happy

Scripture to Memorize: Memorize the John 11:25 scripture (shown right) on page 143.

Lesson Ideas:

Tell children the following: "I want to tell you about a friend of mine." Place an empty chair in the front and tell children to image a special friend sitting in this chair without saying the name "Jesus." Ask children not to say his name until you are through talking about this person. Tell what he did for us using the following:

#1: He created the earth. He created us. He created the animals.

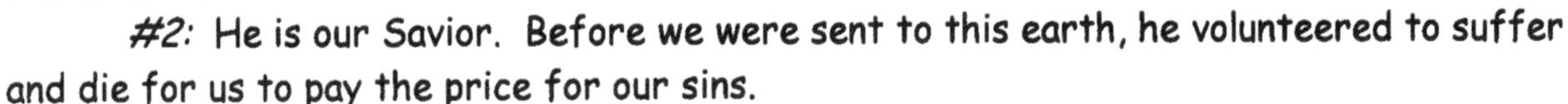

#2: He is our Savior. Before we were sent to this earth, he volunteered to suffer and die for us to pay the price for our sins.

#3: Because of him, we can repent when we do wrong, and we will be forgiven.

#4: Because he was resurrected, we can also be resurrected and live after death.

#5: Because of the Atonement (his suffering and dying for us), we can return to live with him and Heavenly Father, if we follow him.

#6: We can show our thanks to him by praying, reading the scriptures, listening to his servants, the prophets, and obeying the commandments.

#7: Because of him everyone can be resurrected, but not everyone will return to live with Heavenly Father and Jesus unless they repent.

ACTIVITY: Jesus Showed Us That Repentance Can Make Us Happy

(Happy Henry or Miserable Mack Body Building Puzzles)

OBJECTIVE: Help children think about choices Happy Henry and Miserable Mack might make that would make them happy or sad. Explain why it makes them happy to repent, e.g., they don't feel guilty, they know they are choosing the right, the Holy Ghost can be with them to guide them to make choices that will make them happy.

TO MAKE: Mount Henry and Mack signs and body puzzles (pages 145-158) on cardstock paper, laminate, and cut out.

TO PLAY: Tell children, "Jesus showed us that the way to be happy is to repent and choose the right. Let's build a happy boy and a sad boy puzzle to learn how to repent. If we want to be like Happy Henry, we will do as Jesus asked us to do. We will repent of things we have done wrong. If we don't repent, we will be sad like Miserable Mack."

1. Place Happy Henry sign on the right (indicating he will choose the right), and Miserable Mack sign on the left on the board.
2. Place puzzle pieces mixed up in the center of the board.
3. Ask children to come up one at a time, choose a puzzle piece, and read the situation for Henry or Mack. Ask children to tell the others what Happy Henry would do in order to be happy. Tell what Miserable Mack might do that would make him sad.
4. Place puzzle pieces on the board under the signs to build bodies.

THOUGHT TREAT (when appropriate): Fake Frown and Real Smile Cookies: Make two different batches of sugar cookies, one without sugar (replacing salt and flour in place of sugar), and the one with sugar and butter. Cut out the cookie dough with circle cookie cutters. Shape a frown in the one without the sugar and don't frost. Bake. Frost the sweet dough cookies and with contrasting color of frosting, add a smile. Give each child one of each and talk about the difference a sweet smile can make.

BITE SIZE MEMORIZE

I M the resurrection, and the life: he t + + + th in me, though he were R.I.P. yet he live.

John 11:25

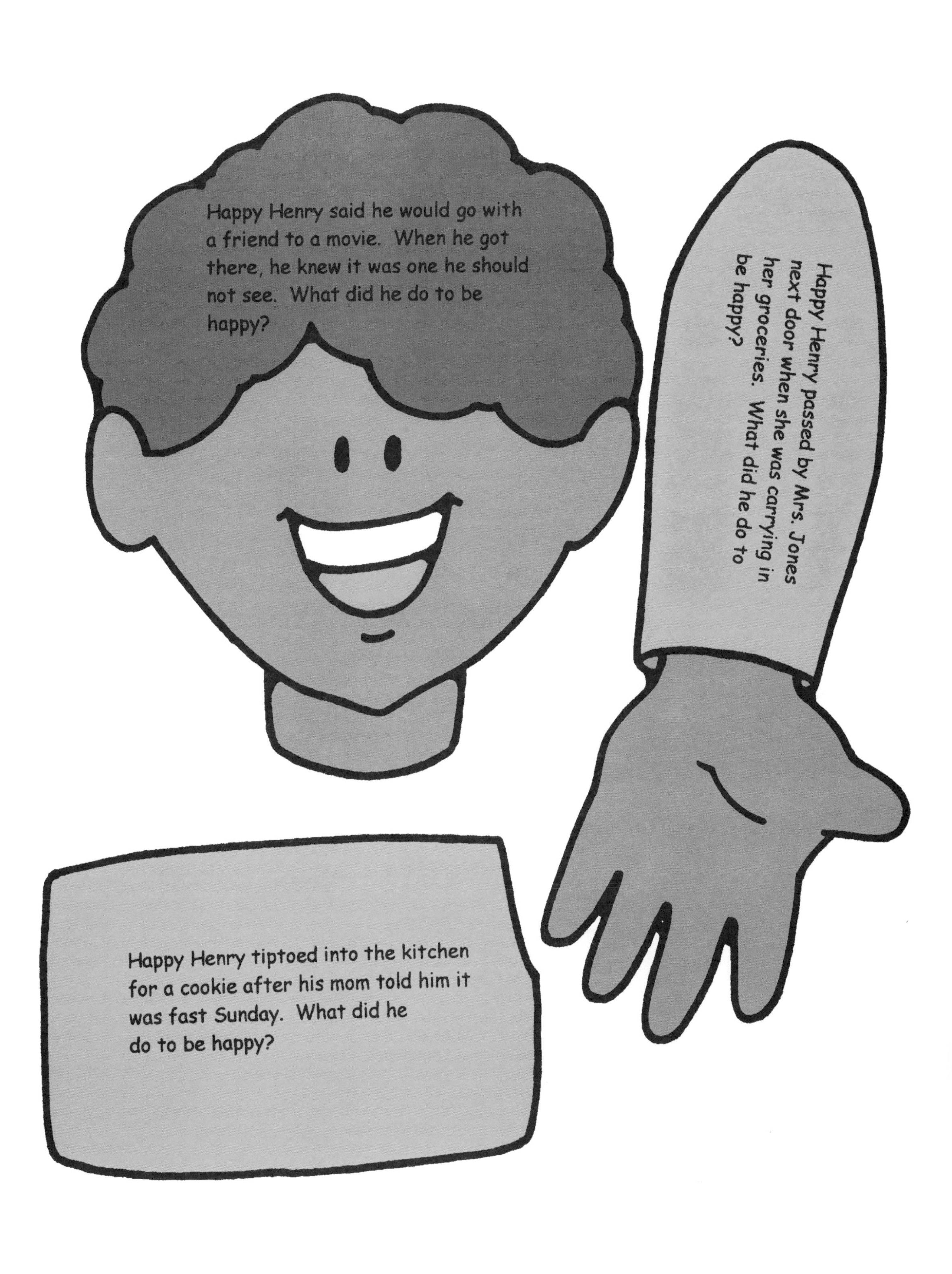
Happy Henry said he would go with a friend to a movie. When he got there, he knew it was one he should not see. What did he do to be happy?
Happy Henry passed by Mrs. Jones next door when she was carrying in her groceries. What did he do to be happy?
Happy Henry tiptoed into the kitchen for a cookie after his mom told him it was fast Sunday. What did he do to be happy?

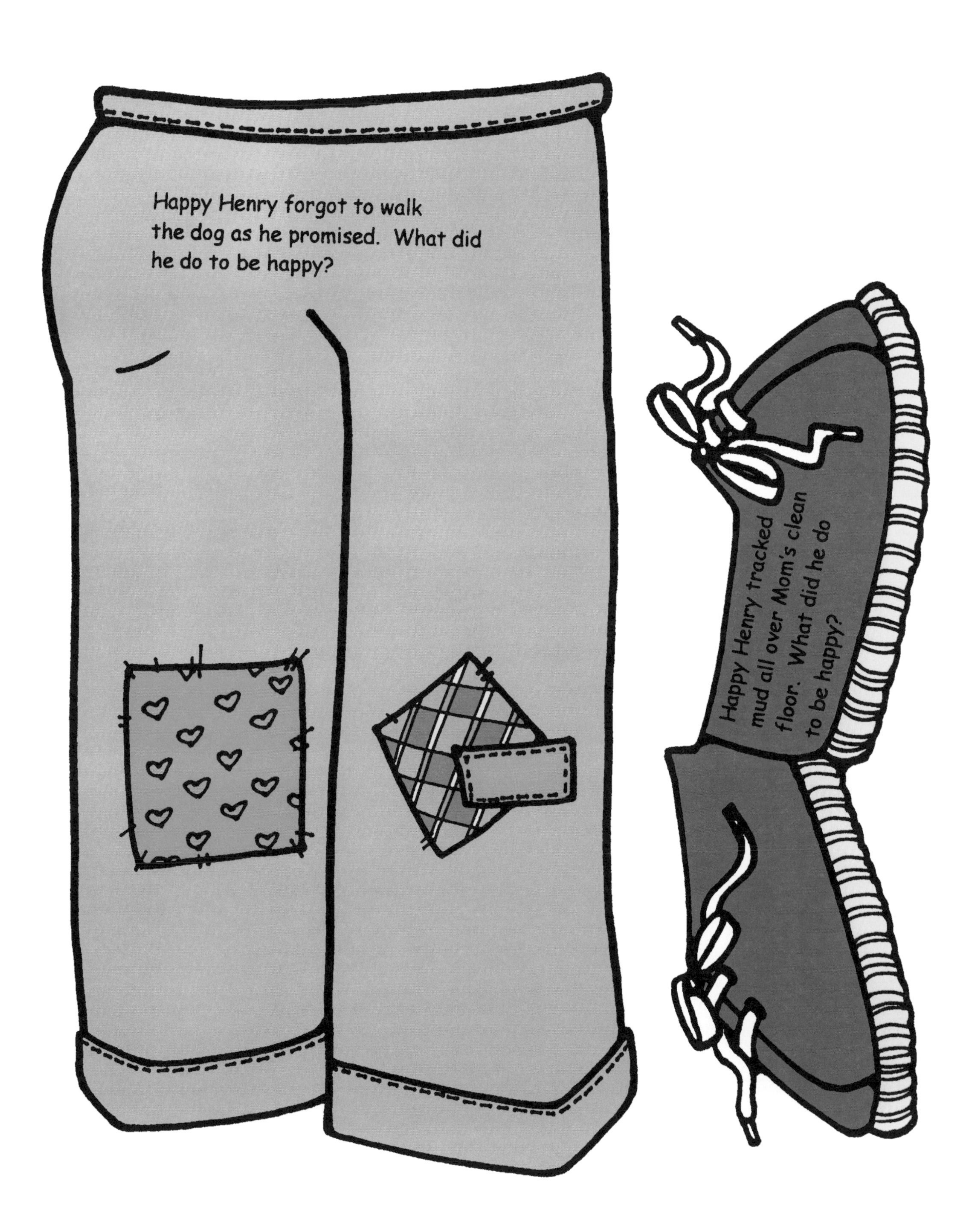
Happy Henry forgot to walk
the dog as he promised. What did
he do to be happy?
Happy Henry tracked
mud all over Mom's clean
floor. What did he do
to be happy?

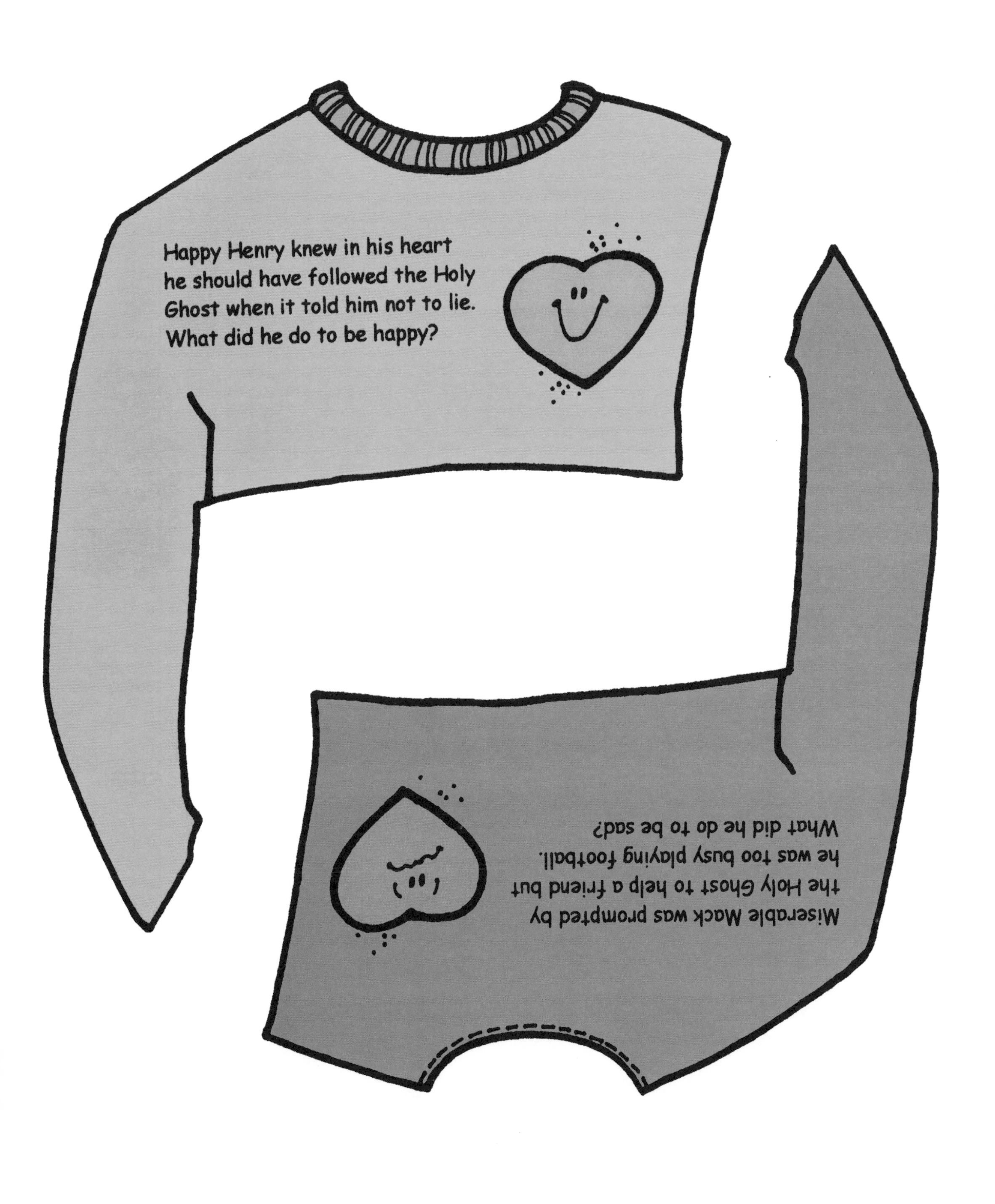
Happy Henry knew in his heart
he should have followed the Holy
Ghost when it told him not to lie.
What did he do to be happy?
Miserable Mack was prompted by
the Holy Ghost to help a friend but
he was too busy playing football.
What did he do to be sad?

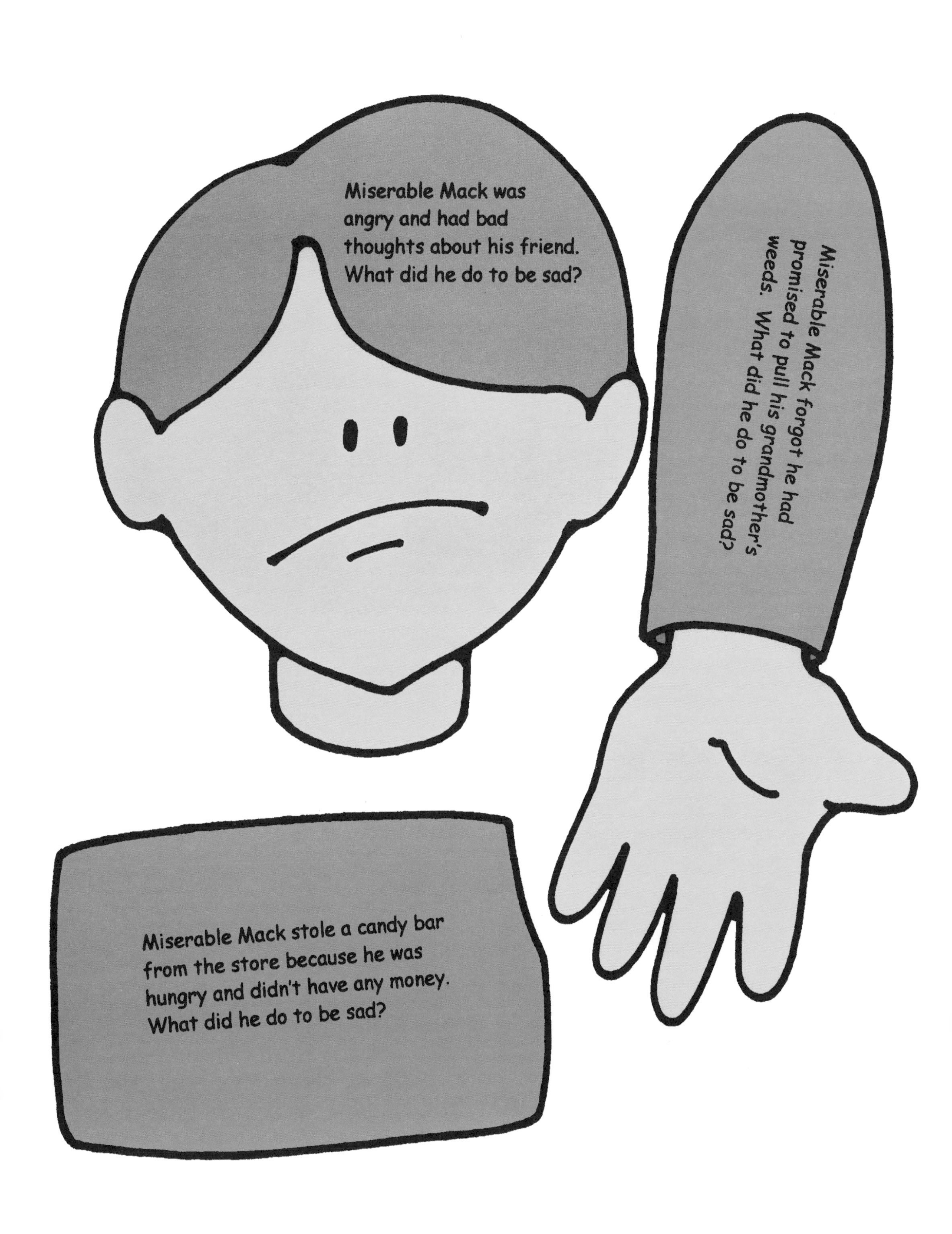
Miserable Mack was angry and had bad thoughts about his friend. What did he do to be sad?
Miserable Mack forgot he had promised to pull his grandmother's weeds. What did he do to be sad?
Miserable Mack stole a candy bar from the store because he was hungry and didn't have any money. What did he do to be sad?

Miserable Mack was late and his
dad asked him to run home right
away. What did he do to be sad?
Miserable Mack's mom
asked him to stop kicking
his brother. What
did he do to be sad?

#10 – Second Coming:

I Will Be Ready to Meet Jesus When He Comes Again

Scripture to Memorize: Memorize the Acts 1:11 scripture (shown right) o page 161.

Lesson Ideas:

QUESTIONS: Ask children the following:

#1: What is the Second Coming? (when Jesus Christ comes again)

#2: What will it be like when Jesus comes again? (Jesus Christ will bring peace, happiness, and love among all righteous people.)

#3: What can I do to prepare for the Second Coming when Jesus will come again? (Have faith and keep his commandments so that we will be ready to receive him when he comes.)

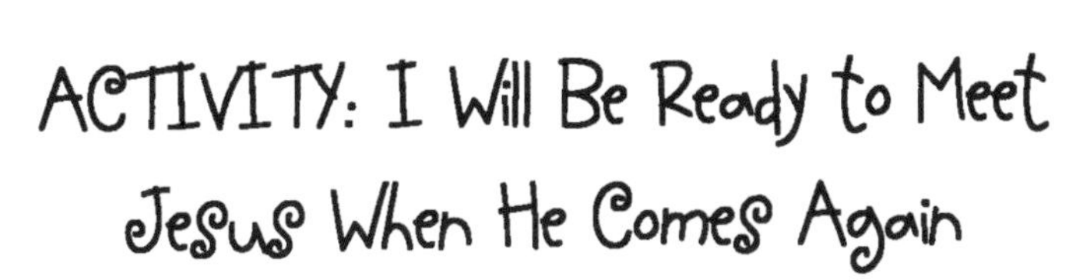

ACTIVITY: I Will Be Ready to Meet Jesus When He Comes Again

(Second Coming Suitcase with Belongings)

OBJECTIVE: Show children how they can prepare to meet Jesus when he comes by packing their personal suitcase with things that will help them be the type of person Jesus would want to meet.

TO MAKE:

1. Mount suitcase parts A and B (page 162-166) on cardstock paper, glue together, laminate and cut out. *Optional:* Cut out first and mount right onto a poster. When cutting out the suitcase, cut a slit at the top of suitcase to insert items as you talk about them (gluing only the sides to a poster paper so the pocket remains open).

2. Mount suitcase items (pages 167-172) on cardstrock paper, laminate, and cut out.
3. Place suitcase items on the wall next to suitcase or around the room.

TO PACK SUITCASE:
Tell children, "We are getting ready for a special day when Jesus Christ comes back to the earth. He wants us to be ready, so let's pack our bags."
1. Ask children one at a time to come up and find an item they could pack in their Second Coming suitcase.
2. Ask the child to read the message and talk about why this item would be important to pack (how it will prepare them to meet Jesus when he comes again), e.g., a pair of pants with patches on the knee to remind the child to "kneel in prayer."

THOUGHT TREAT (when appropriate): Apple to remind children to keep the word of wisdom (a symbol shown above they can pack in their Second Coming Suitcase).

BITE SIZE MEMORIZE

↑ Cut carefully along the inside of the dotted line. ↑

Do not cut on the dotted line. Use this margin to mount the other side.

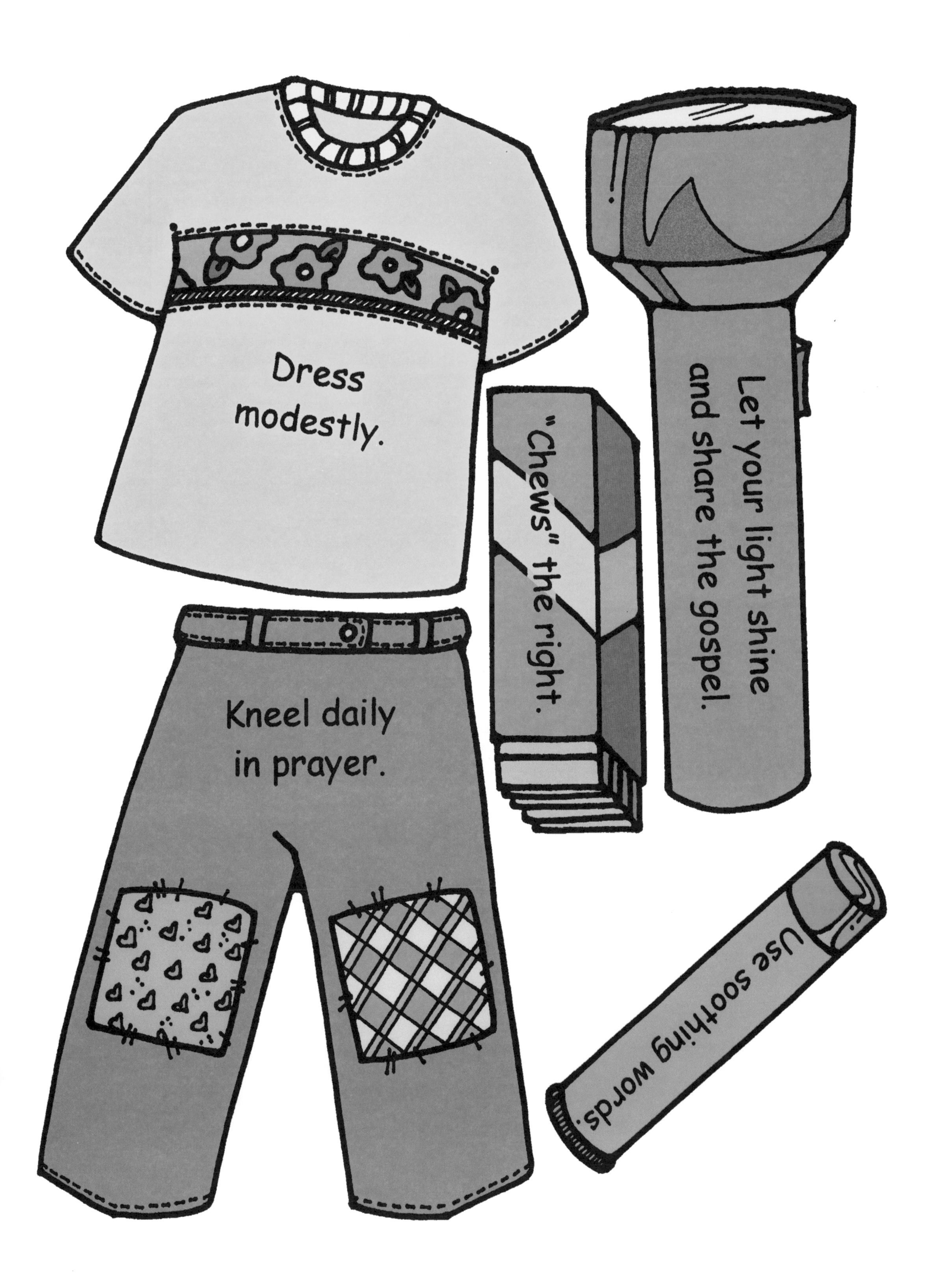

Dress modestly.
Kneel daily in prayer.
"Chews" the right.
Let your light shine and share the gospel.
Use soothing words.

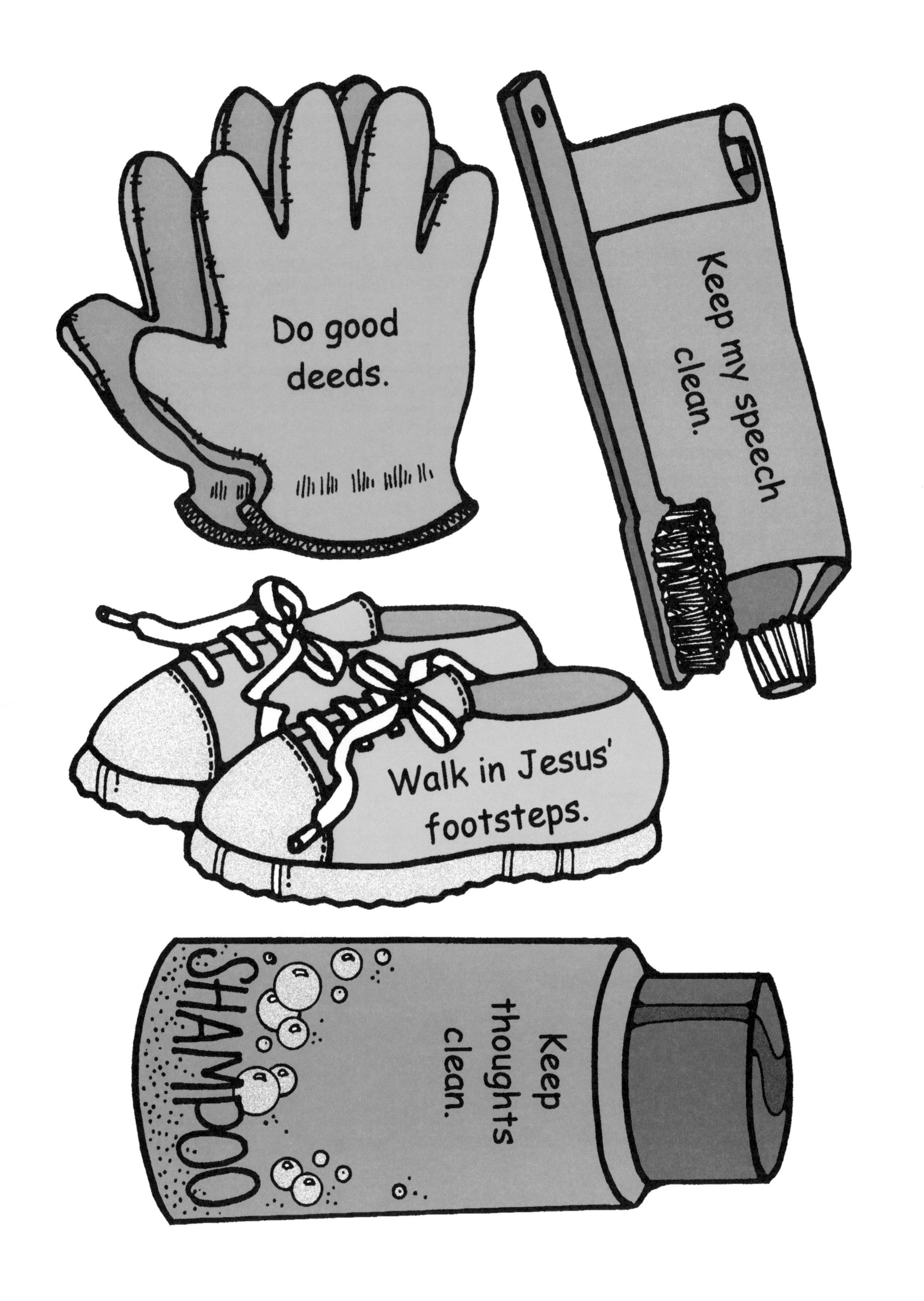

Do good deeds.
Keep my speech clean.
Walk in Jesus' footsteps.
SHAMPOO
Keep thoughts clean.

Obey Word of Wisdom.
GRANOLA
Prepare food storage.
Read scriptures.
Pay tithing.
Repent to stay clean.
Attend church.

#11 – Service: I Will Love and Serve Others

BITE SIZE MEMORIZE

thou an Xample of the [bee]+[leaf]+rs, in word, in conversation, in [chair]+ity, in [spoon]+it, in faith, in purity.

I Timothy 4:12

Scripture to Memorize: Memorize the Timothy 4:12 scripture (shown right) on page 175.

Lesson Ideas:

QUESTION: Ask "How can we love and serve others?" and answer the question using the following scriptures and Primary lessons to teach:

#1: We can be a good example (Luke 22:32, 3 Nephi 18:24, *Primary 1*, lesson 36, *Primary 3*, lesson 45, *Primary 6*, lesson 26).

#2: We can love and serve others (1 John 3:18; 4:21, Mosiah 2:17; 18:8-10, *Primary 2,* lesson 39).

#3: We can forgive one another (Matthew 18:23-35, 3 Nephi 13:14-15, Doctrine and Covenants 6:9-10; 98:40, *Primary 3*, lesson 23, *Primary 6*, lesson 17).

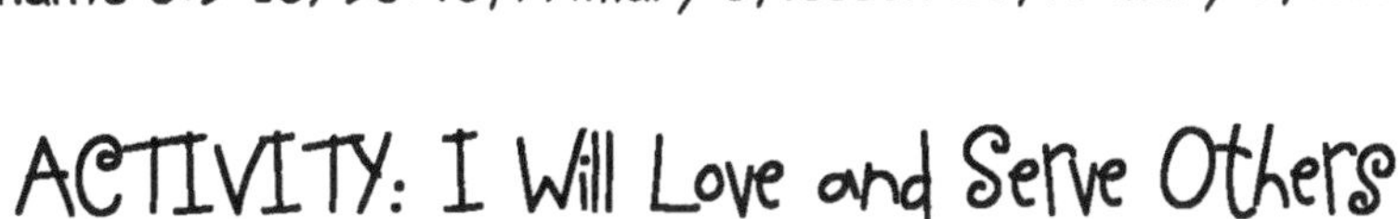

(My Service Garden Game to Plant Acts of Service)

OBJECTIVE: Help children learn how to show love to others by serving them.

TO MAKE: Mount garden sign, fruit and vegetable puzzle pieces (pages 177-192) on cardstock paper, laminate, and cut out.

TO SET-UP GAME:

1. Place the "My Service Garden" sign on the board in the bottom center.
2. Divide the garden fruit and vegetables in half, e.g., placing half the carrot in pile #1 and the other half of the carrot in pile #2.
3. Draw a vertical line in the center of the garden/board to divide teams.
4. Divide pile #1 in half and place 12 half pieces on the left side of the board and 12 half pieces on the right side of the board.
5. Place pile #2 in one container for both teams to draw from.
6. Have tape ready to stick on back of produce pieces as children place them on the board.

INTRODUCE GAME: Tell children that if they plant acts of service each day they will reap a harvest of blessings from Heavenly Father. It's easy to say "I love you," to your family or that "I like you" to a friend, but they don't know you love them unless you show them through service. In 1 John 3:18 we read, *"My little children, let us not love in word, neither in tongue; but in deed and in truth."* In our garden we don't want to grow weeds so let's plant good deeds of service (point to sign).

TO PLAY GAME:

1. Divide children into two teams.
2. Point to the board where produce is set up (see #4 above).
3. Teams take turns drawing a produce piece from the container to make a match
4. If they draw a produce piece that matches one in their garden, they place it in their garden to complete the produce and read what the fruit or vegetable reads.
5. If team draws a match for the other team, they place the item back in the container and their turn is over.
6. The first team to complete their service garden wins! Finish the other team matches and read examples.

THOUGHT TREAT (when appropriate): Prepare and cut up a variety of fruits and vegetables and review the garden visuals.

 All images can be printed in color or black and white, using the *Gospel Fun Activities* CD-ROM.

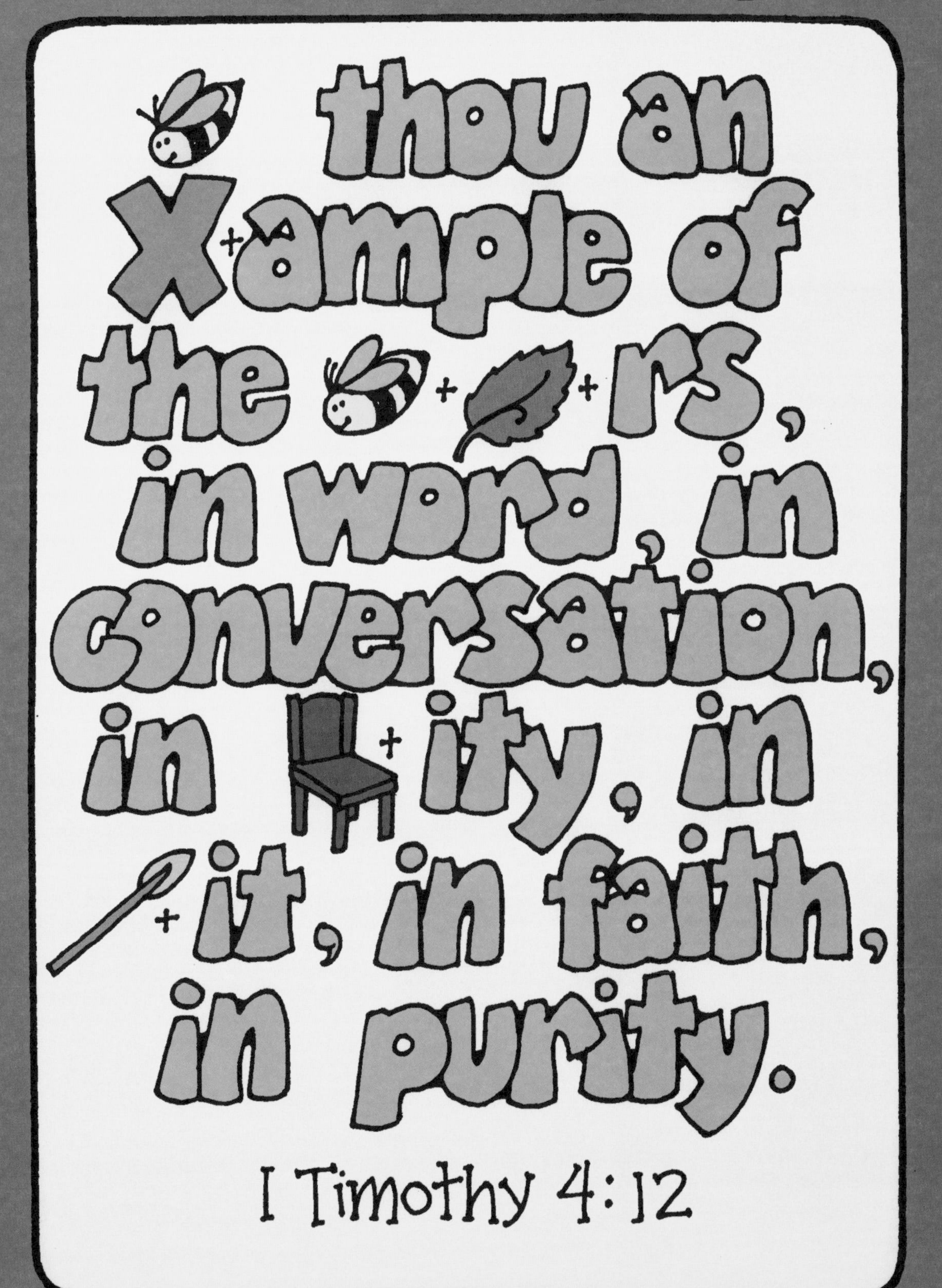
BITE SIZE MEMORIZE
thou an
Xample of
the + + rs,
in word, in
conversation,
in + ity, in
+ it, in faith,
in purity.
I Timothy 4:12

My
Service
Garden
Don't grow weeds,
Plant good deeds!

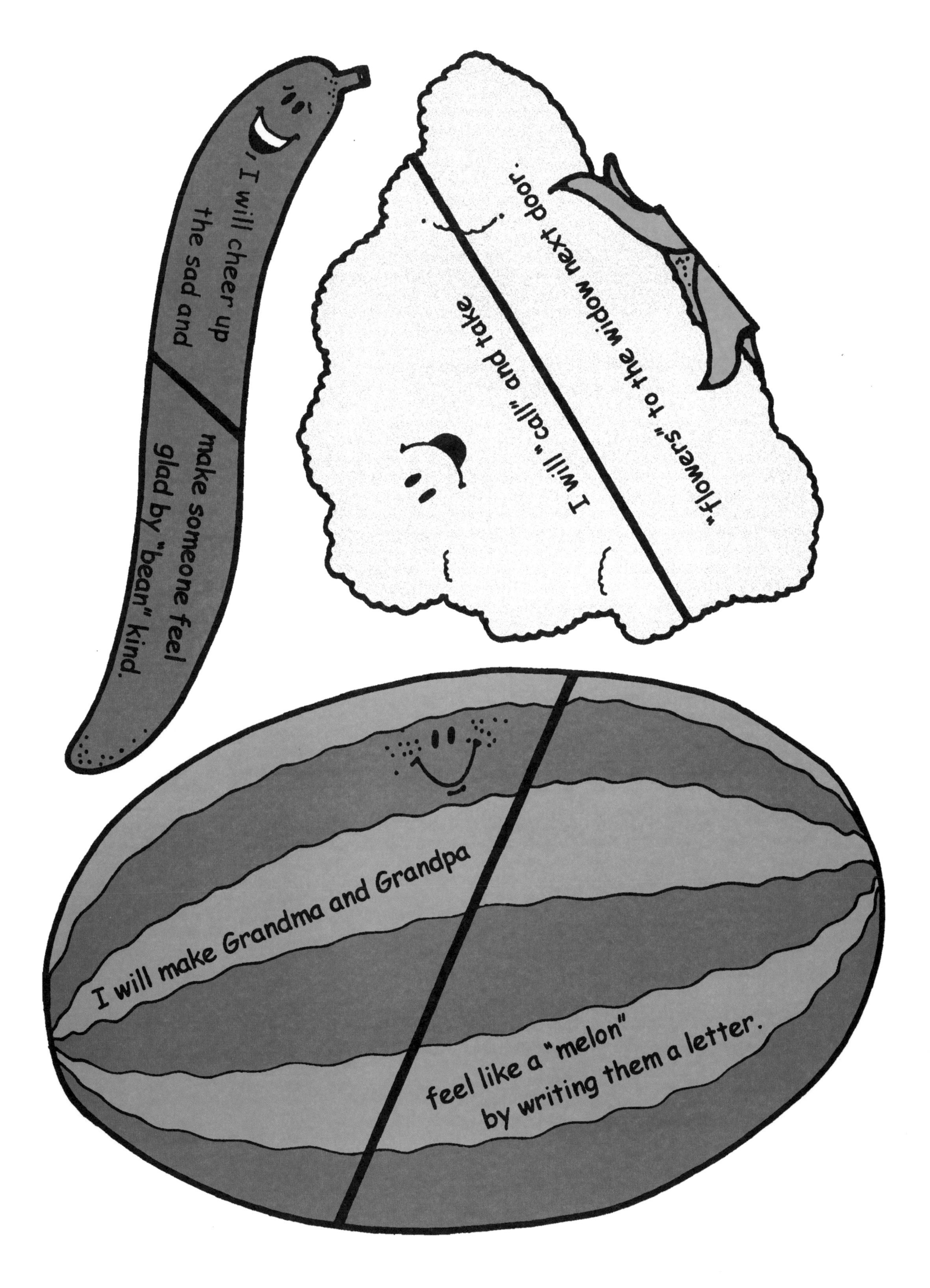

I will cheer up
the sad and
make someone feel
glad by "bean" kind.
I will "call" and take
"flowers" to the widow next door.
I will make Grandma and Grandpa
feel like a "melon"
by writing them a letter.

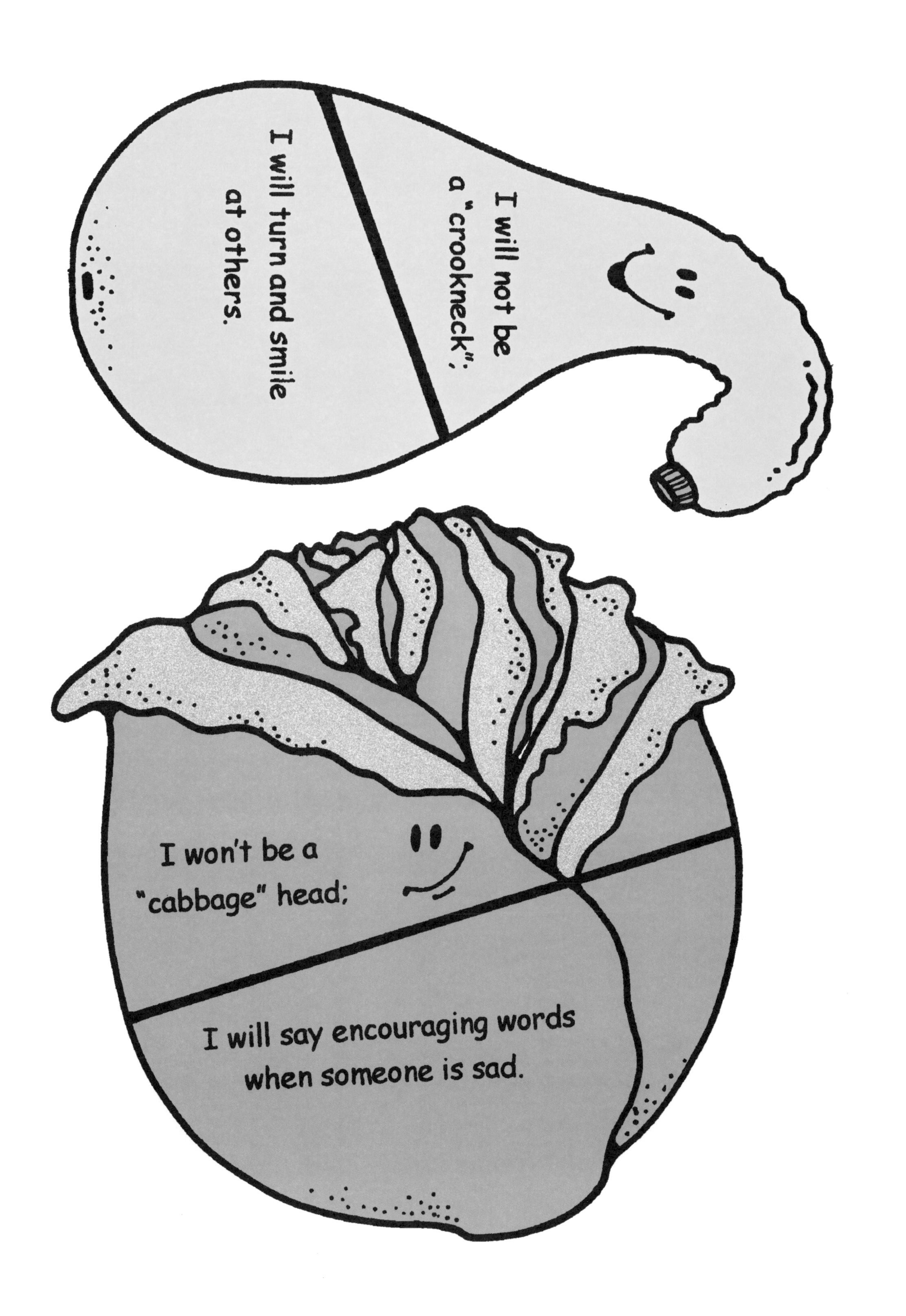
I will not be
a "crookneck";
I will turn and smile
at others.
I won't be a
"cabbage" head;
I will say encouraging words
when someone is sad.

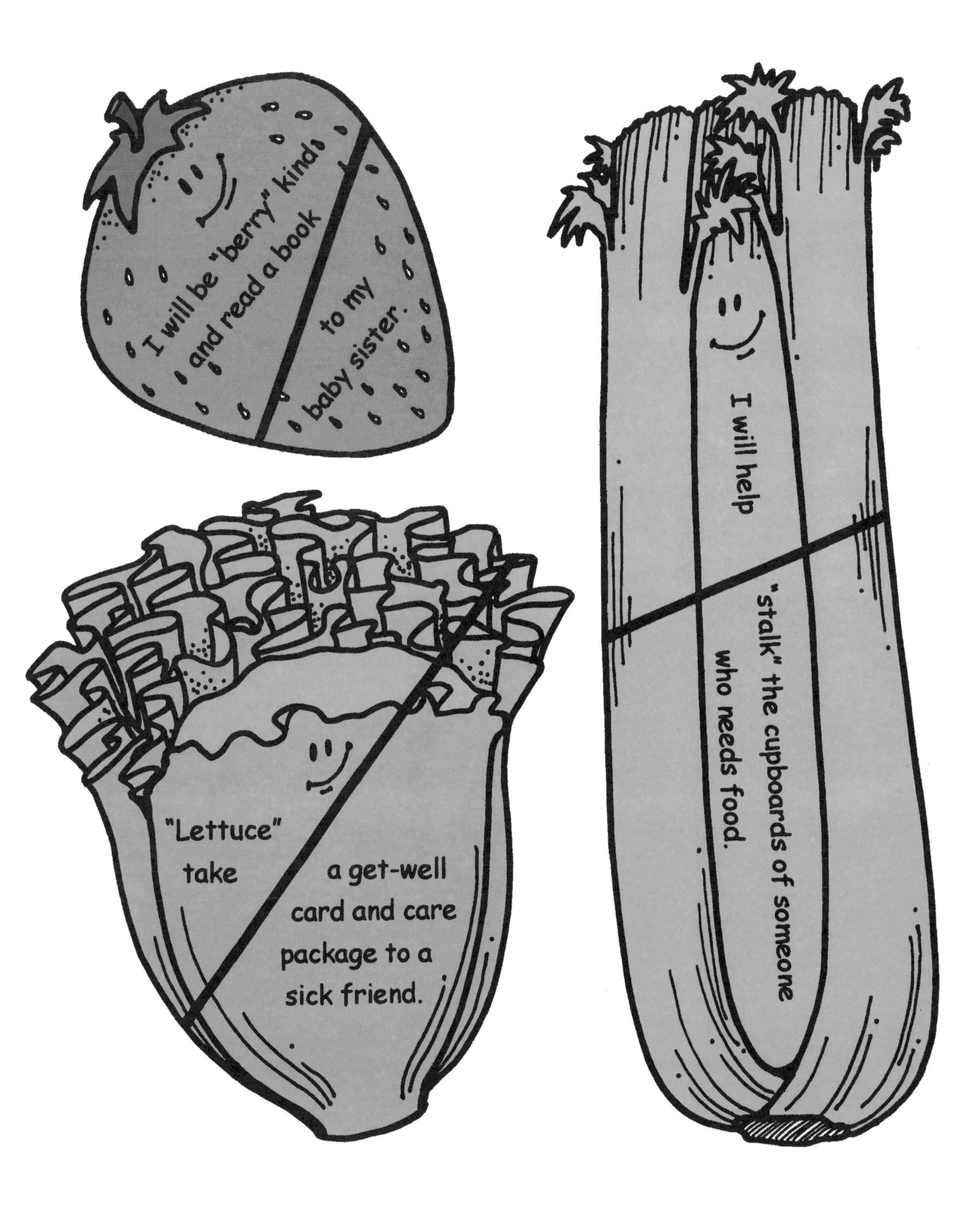
I will be "berry" kind and read a book
to my baby sister.
"Lettuce" take
a get-well card and care package to a sick friend.
I will help
"stalk" the cupboards of someone who needs food.

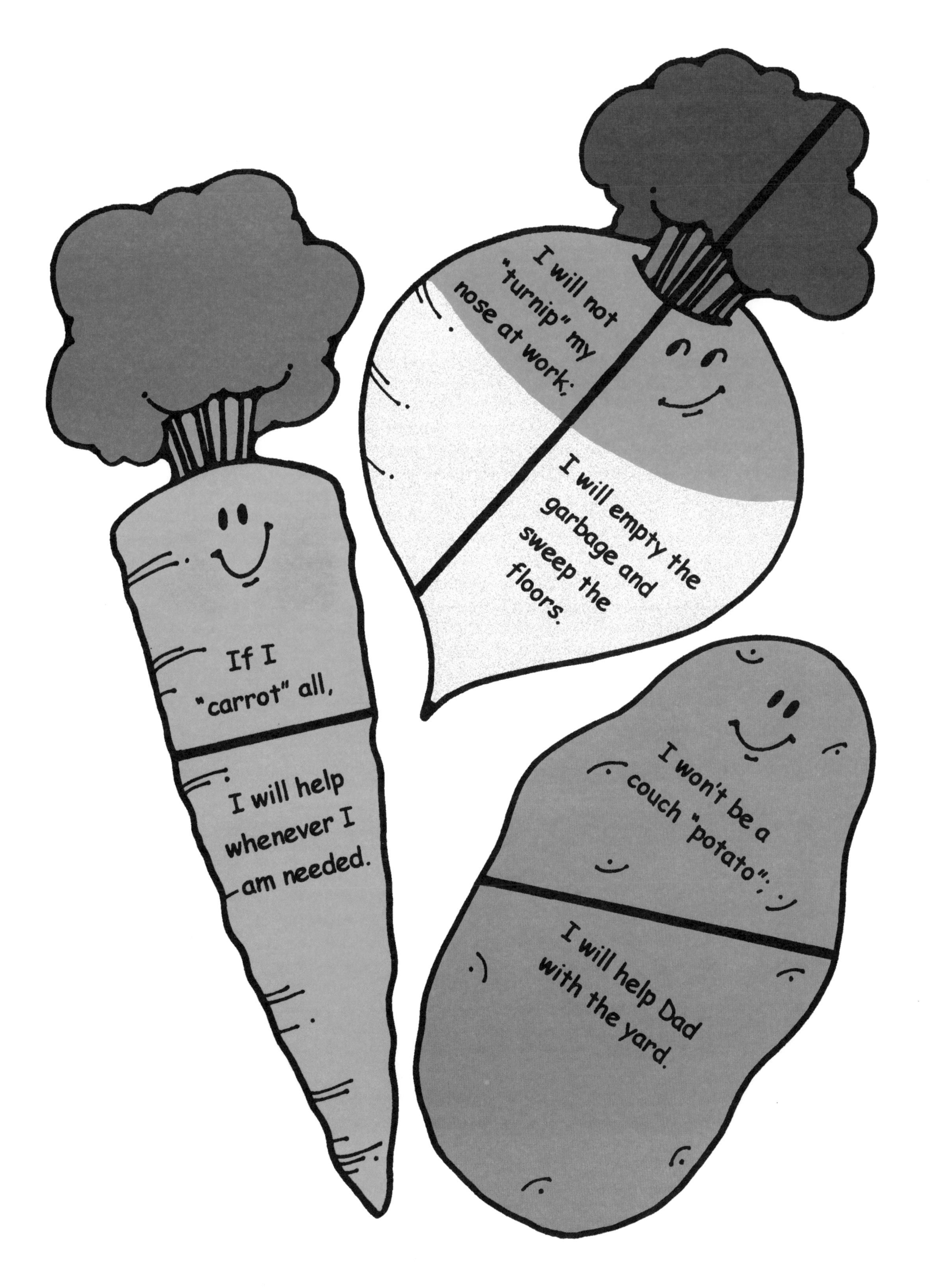
I will not "turnip" my nose at work;
I will empty the garbage and sweep the floors.
If I "carrot" all,
I will help whenever I am needed.
I won't be a couch "potato";
I will help Dad with the yard.

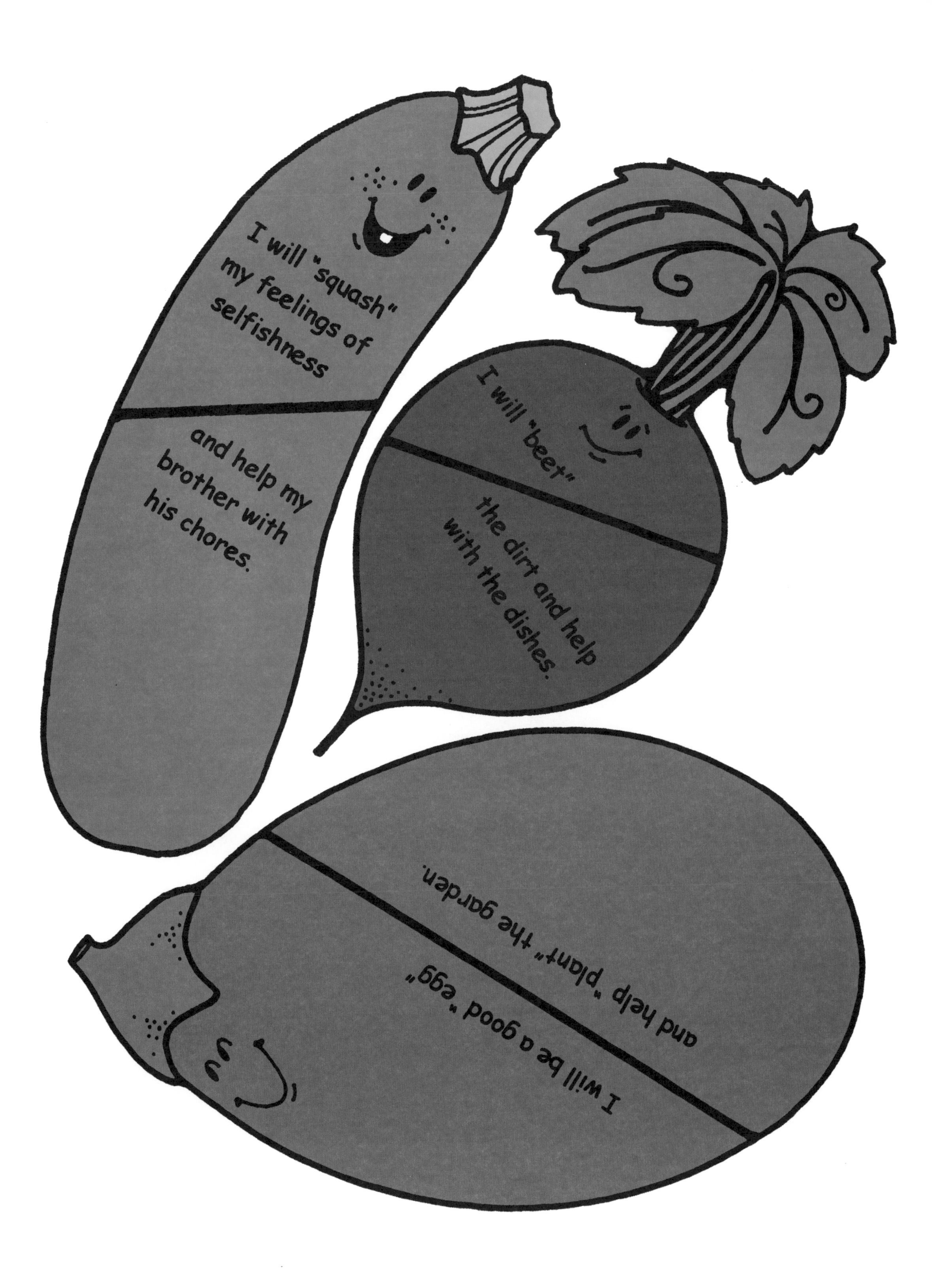
I will "squash" my feelings of selfishness
and help my brother with his chores.
I will "beet"
the dirt and help with the dishes.
I will be a good "egg"
and help "plant" the garden.

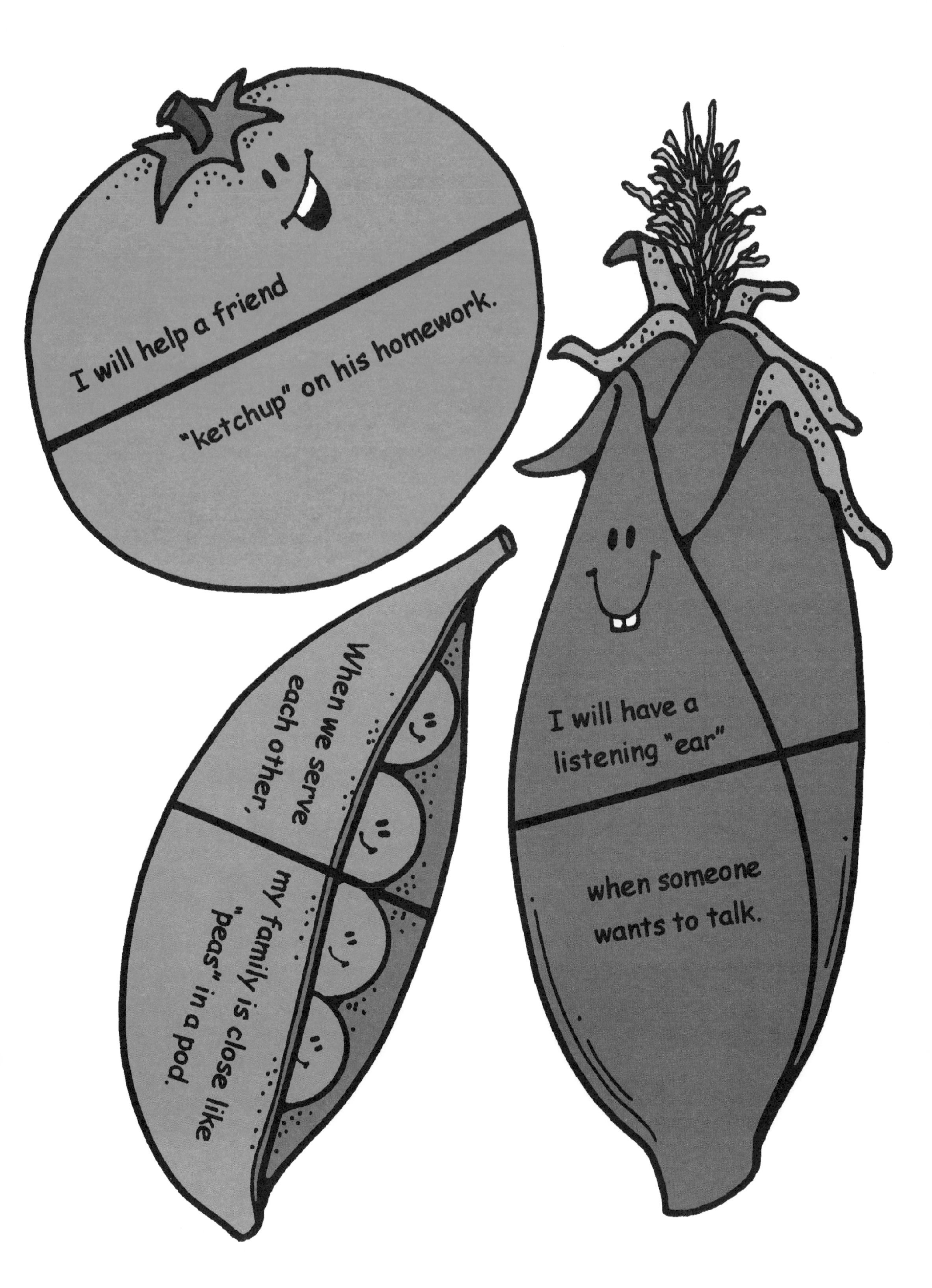

I will help a friend
"ketchup" on his homework.
When we serve
each other,
my family is close like
"peas" in a pod.
I will have a
listening "ear"
when someone
wants to talk.

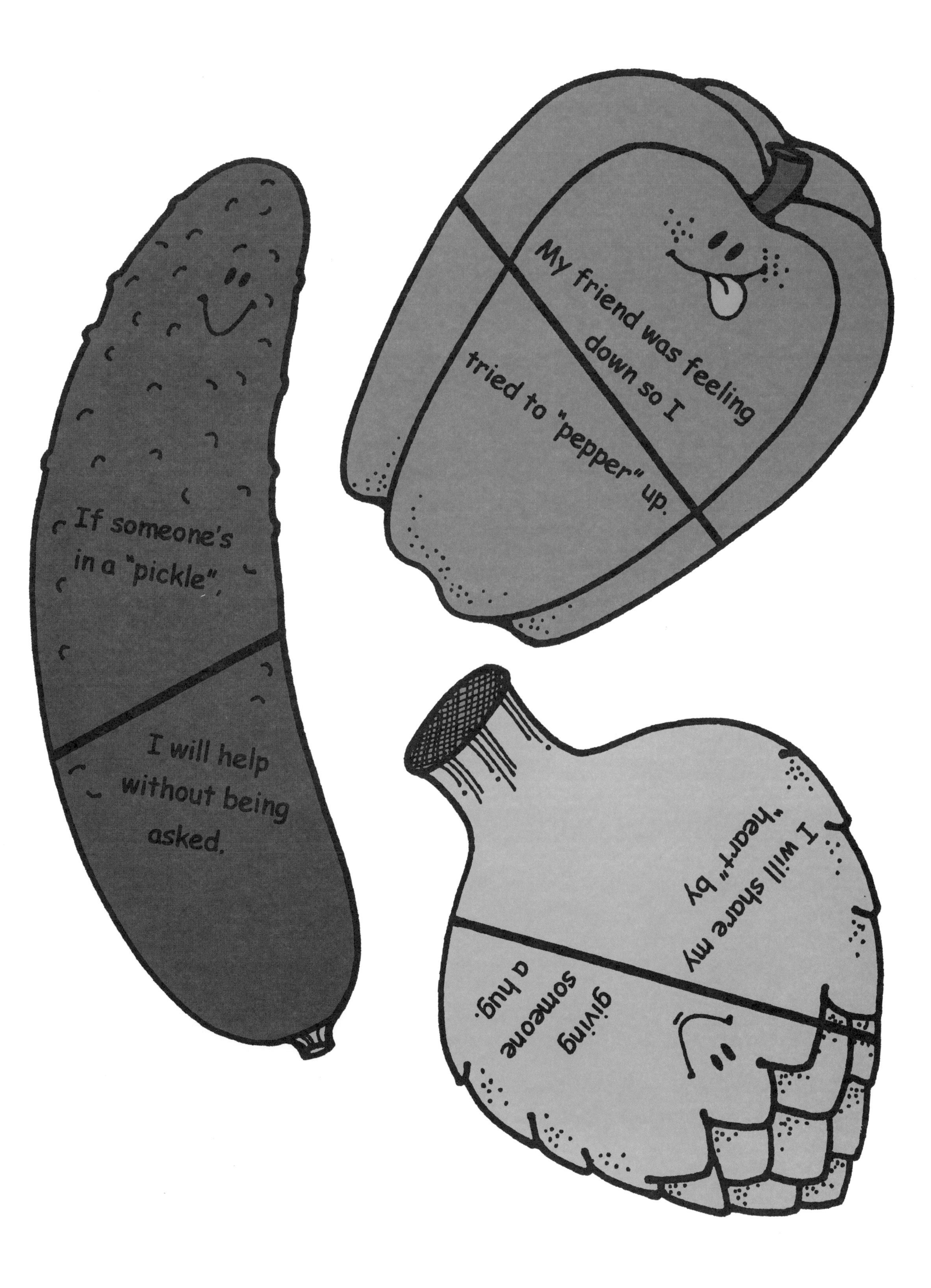
If someone's in a "pickle",
I will help without being asked.
My friend was feeling down so I
tried to "pepper" up.
I will share my "heart" by
giving someone a hug.

#12 – Testimony:

I Will Build My House Upon the Rock—Jesus Christ

Scripture to Memorize: Memorize the Helaman 5:12 scripture (shown right) on page 195.

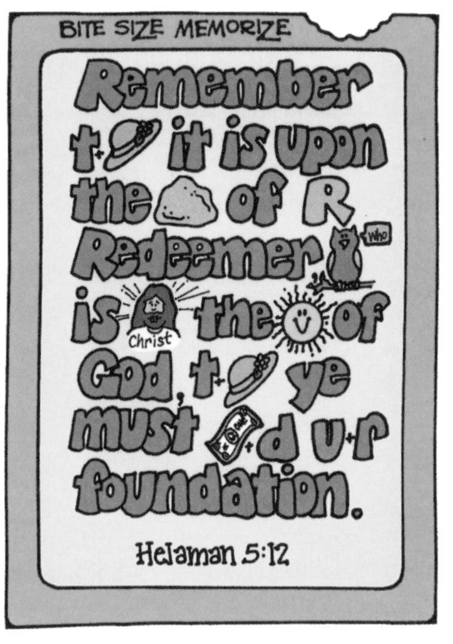

Lesson Ideas:

QUESTIONS: Ask children the following:

#1: What Is a Testimony? (knowing that Heavenly Father lives, Jesus Christ is the Savior and Redeemer, Joseph Smith is the prophet who restored the true Church, the Book of Mormon is the word of God, and we have a living prophet who guides us.

#2: How Do We Gain a Testimony? (pray, read scriptures, keep commandments, and follow the living prophets)

#3: How Is a Testimony Given to Us? (through the Holy Ghost)

#4: What Feelings Do We Have in Our Heart when the Holy Ghost testifies that things are true? (warm feeling, comforting feeling, peaceful feeling, happy feeling)

#5: How Does Our Testimony Grow? (Share it with others during testimony meeting and when prompted by the Spirit to bear your testimony. Also, continue reading the scriptures, keeping the commandments, and following the prophet.)

ACTIVITY: I Will Build My House Upon the Rock (Jesus Christ)

(Testimony Rocks to Build a Sure Foundation)

OBJECTIVE: Help children share their testimony of the gospel from key words written on testimony rocks. *Scriptures:* 3 Nephi 11:40, Matthew 7:24-27, and Helaman 5:12

TO MAKE:

1. Mount house parts A and B (pages 195-200) onto cardstock paper or onto a poster and laminate. If not mounting house on a poster, cut out house and glue together then laminate.
2. Mount rocks (pages 201-210) onto cardstock paper, laminate, and cut out.
3. Tape rocks around the room, and tape house on the board.

INTRODUCE ACTIVITY:

1. Tell children about the wise man and the foolish man (Matthew 7:24-27 and Helaman 5:12). Then sing the song "The Wise Man and the Foolish Man" (page 281) in the *Children's Songbook*.
2. See Primary 2-CTR A lesson #36 (pp. 194-195) for lesson ideas.

PRESENT ACTIVITY:

1. Ask children one at a time to find a rock (placed around the room) and read it aloud.
2. Have children say how this testimony rock can help them build a sure foundation.
3. Have children place their rock below the house.
4. Explain the following: "When the rocks are placed under a house, they create a strong foundation and the rain can't wash it away. We can create a strong foundation by doing things that strengthen our testimony in Jesus Christ."

THOUGHT TREAT (when appropriate): Graham Cracker House. Give each child a large graham cracker and a tube of frosting to draw and decorate their own house, or do this ahead of time, using ½ graham cracker for each child. Talk about building a strong house by following Jesus. Talk about things Jesus has asked us to do to build a strong foundation to our house. Review the words written on the rocks and talk about each, sharing experiences.

 All images can be printed in color or black and white, using the *Gospel Fun Activities* CD-ROM.

BITE SIZE MEMORIZE

Remember t+ it is upon
the of R
Redeemer who,
is Christ the of
God, t+ ye
must +d u+r
foundation.

Helaman 5:12

Cut carefully along the inside of the dotted line.

Do not cut on the dotted line. Use this margin to mount the other side.
Foundation

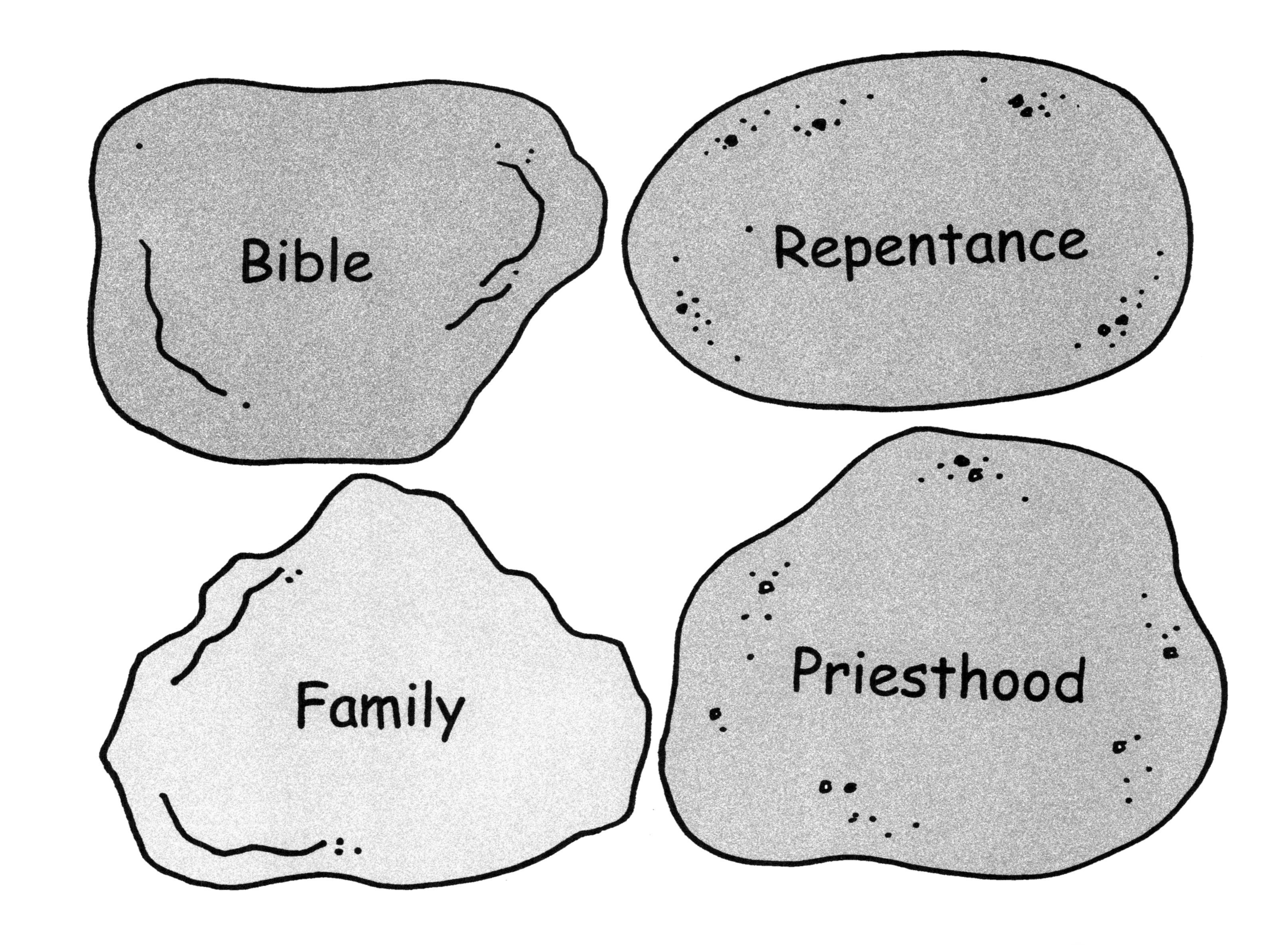
Bible
Repentance
Family
Priesthood

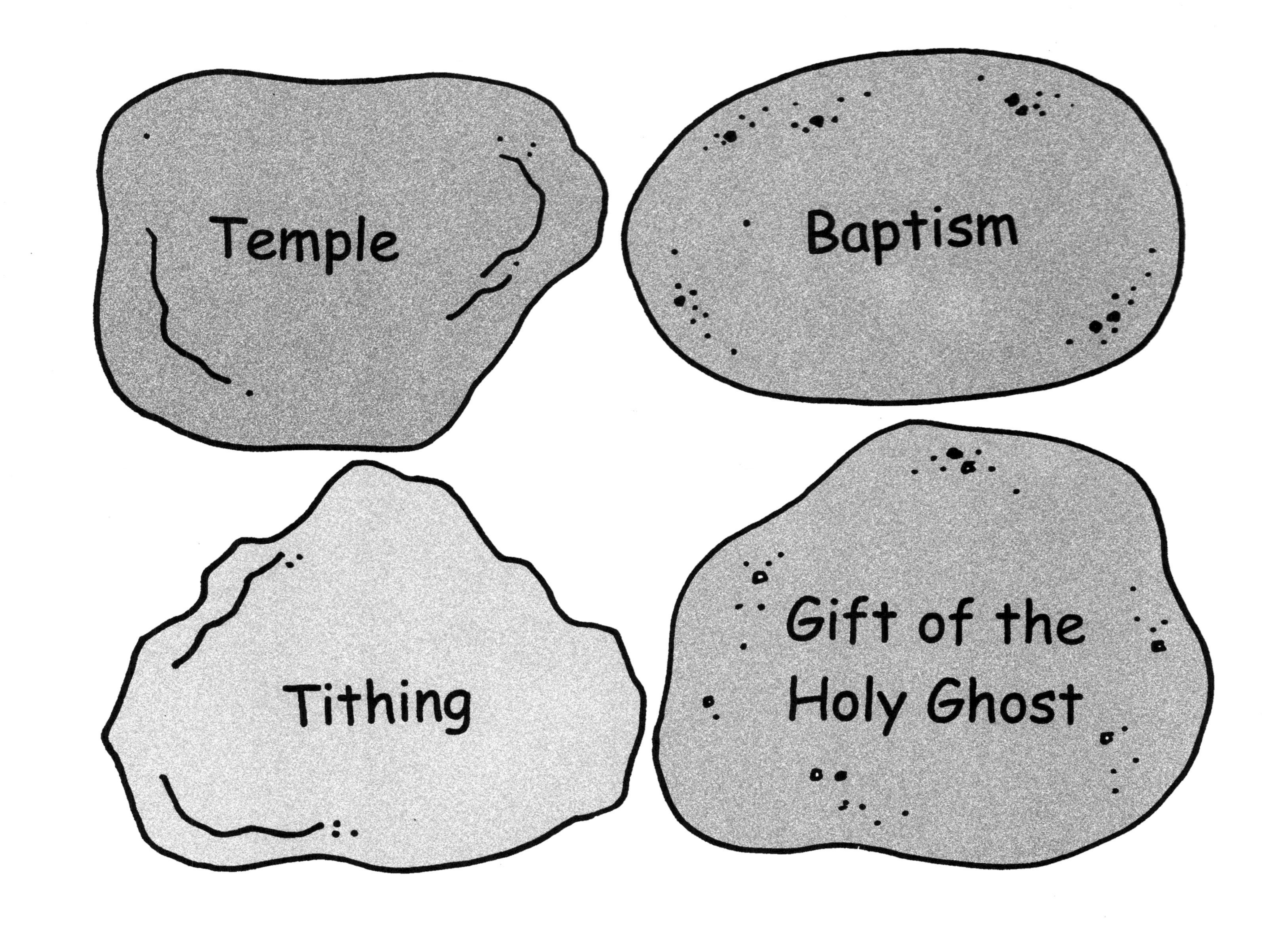
Temple
Baptism
Tithing
Gift of the
Holy Ghost

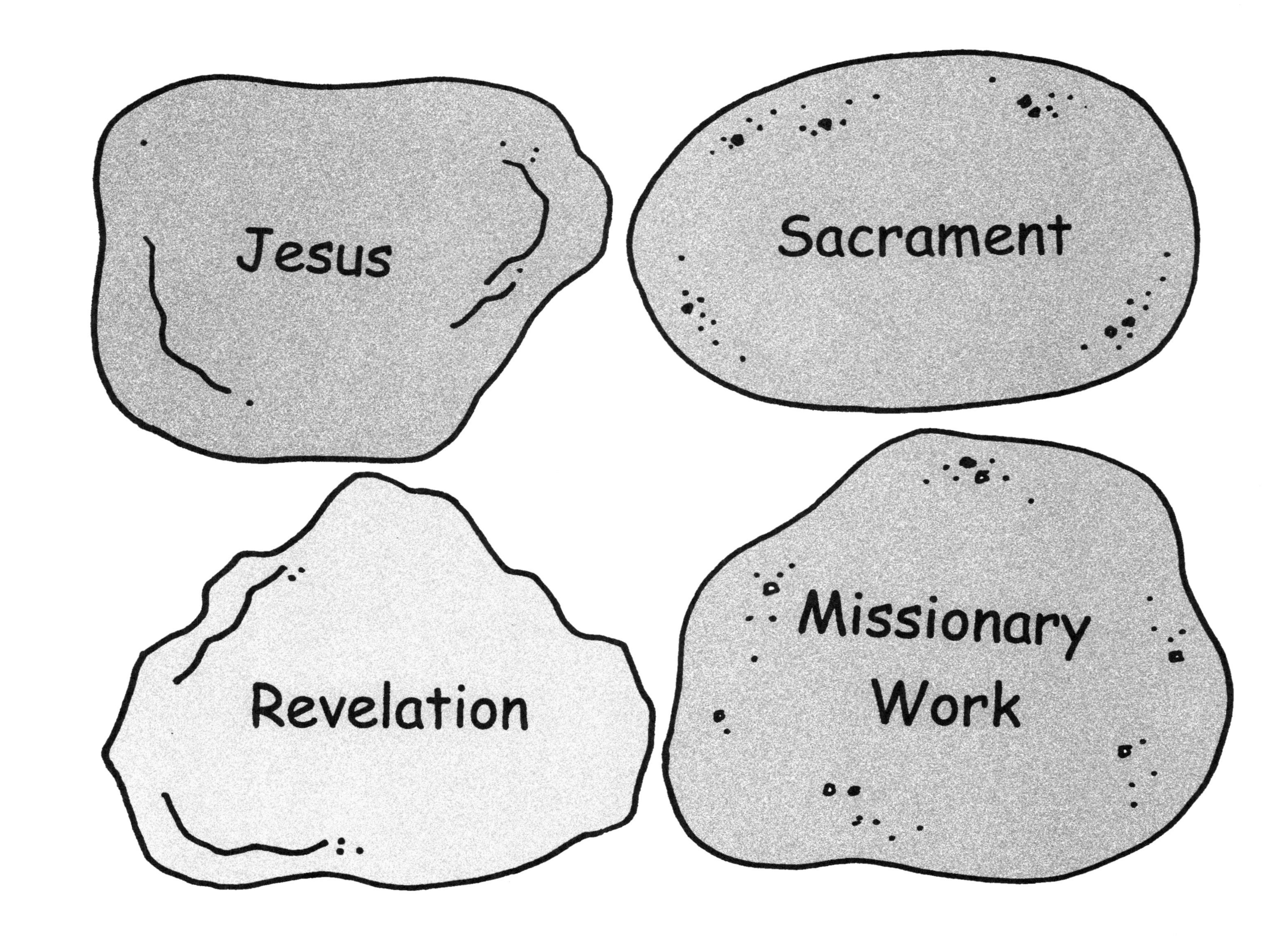
Jesus
Sacrament
Revelation
Missionary Work

Heavenly
Father
Service
Love
Prayer

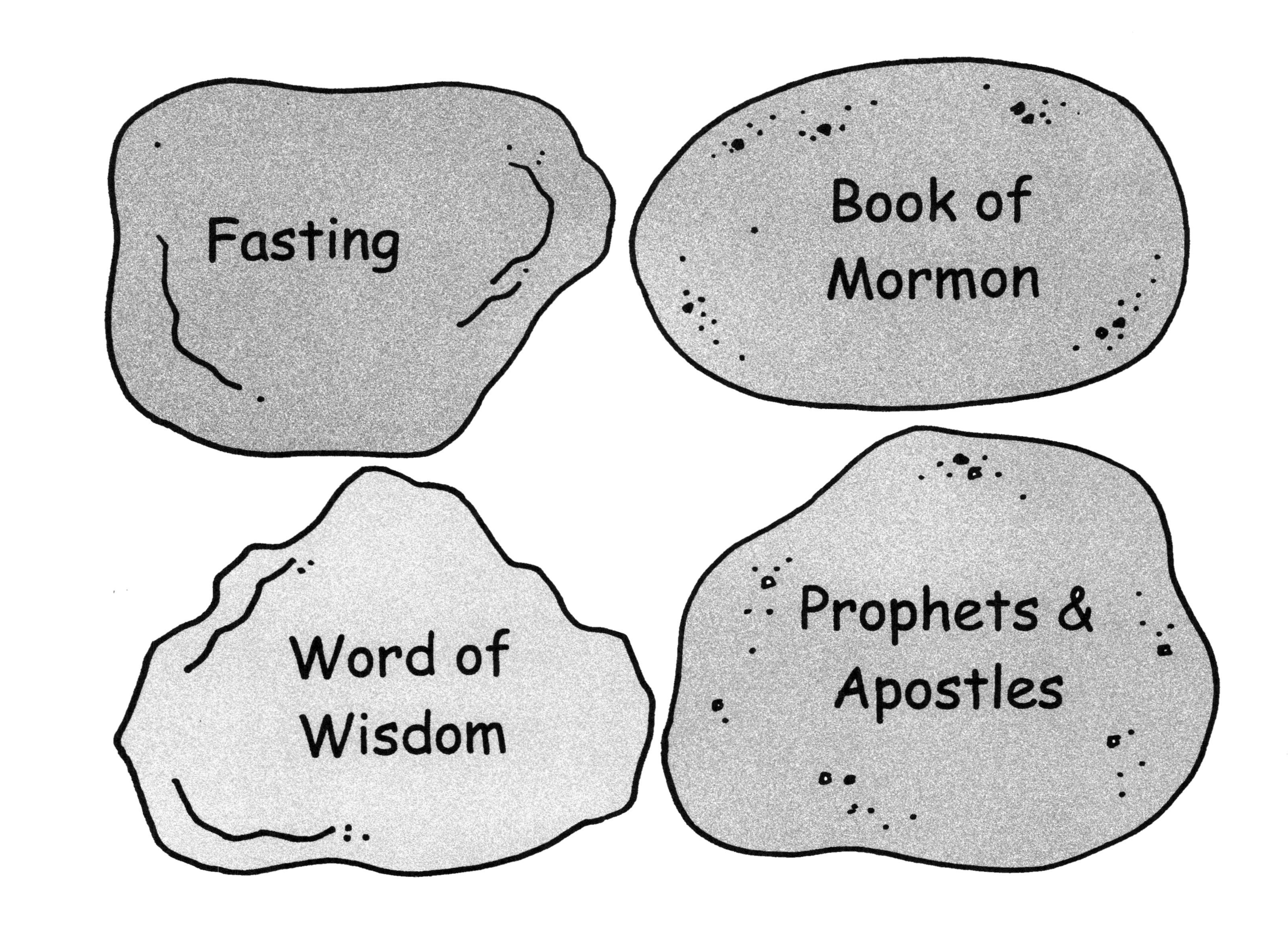
Fasting
Book of
Mormon
Word of
Wisdom
Prophets &
Apostles

Quick-and-Easy Ways to Achievement Days
for Girls Ages 8-11

The Church's Achievement Days program is made easier with these 24 goal activities to help girls ages 8-11, achieve goals in 12 twelve areas, including Arts and Crafts, Education and Scholarship, Family History, Family Skills, Health and Personal Grooming, Hospitality, Outdoor Fun and Skills, Personal Preparedness, Safety and Emergency Preparedness, Service and Citizenship, Spirituality, Sports and Physical Fitness.

Following detailed lesson plans, girls can create a Super Study Spot Pad for their desk, make a Best Friends First-Aid Kit, spotlight their ancestors, plan a fire escape route from their home, do activities with the elderly, make a Sabbath Day Activity Box—and on and on!

These activities and patterns are available in the book and CD-ROM to print images in full color or black and white.

With *Quick-and-Easy Ways to Achievement Days* you can whip up an activity in minutes to train pre-teen girls, or even boys to prepare themselves for life's challenges.

Preview of

Super Singing Activities

Full-color, Ready-to-use Visuals to Motivate Children to Sing

There is never a dull moment in Primary singing time and family home evening with these *Super Singing Activities*. Children will look forward to these singing time activities that encourage them to sing in a variety of ways. Use them each week along with the *Primary Partners Singing Fun!* book and CD-ROM to match the sharing time theme for the current year.

With these ready-to-use visuals you will save time and money, as the visuals are colored for you. The pages are perforated, ready to tear out and use. Simply cut them out and you're on your way to making singing time fun.

This book of visual activities is also available to print in color and black and white from CD-ROM (shown right).

Some of the Super Singing Activities Are: Melody's Family Tree (shown right), Bird in the Leafy Treetops, Build a Snowman, Christmas Tree Sing with Me, City of Enoch Singing Meter, Fill Noah's Ark Pick-a-song, Name That Tune, Singing Simon, Sunny Sunday Sounds, Temple Flowers "Bee" a Singer, Animal and Insect Do as I'm Doing, Go Fishing.